DISTRIBUTIVE JUSTICE

This book presents a critical appraisal of the main theories of distributive justice. It develops the view that all such theories, or at least all liberal theories, may be seen as expressions of laissez-faire with compensations for factors that they consider to be morally arbitrary.

More precisely, these theories are interpreted as specifying that the outcome of individuals acting independently, without the intervention of any central authority, is just, provided that those who fare ill for reasons that the theories deem to be arbitrary, for example, because they have fewer talents than others, receive compensation from those who fare well. The principal theories discussed are Rawls's justice as fairness, Dworkin's equality of resources, what may loosely be called Steiner–Vallentyne common ownership theories, and Nozick's entitlements theory.

The book considers the extent, if any, to which the theories examined can accommodate both liberty and equality. It concludes that if any such accommodation is possible it will be found in common ownership theories.

Michael Allingham is a Fellow of Magdalen College, Oxford.

DISTRIBUTIVE JUSTICE

Michael Allingham

Routledge
Taylor & Francis Group

LONDON AND NEW YORK

First published 2014
by Routledge
2 Park Square, Milton Park, Abingdon, Oxon OX14 4RN

and by Routledge
711 Third Avenue, New York, NY 10017

Routledge is an imprint of the Taylor & Francis Group, an informa business

© 2014 Michael Allingham

British Library Cataloguing in Publication Data
A catalogue record for this book is available from the British Library

Library of Congress Cataloging in Publication Data
   Distributive justice / Michael Allingham.
      pages cm
   Summary: "This book presents a critical appraisal of the main theories of distributive justice. Theories are explored that seek to specify what is meant by a just distribution of goods among members of society. It does so in a framework in which all liberal theories of justice are seen as expressions of laissez-faire with compensations for factors that they consider being morally arbitrary. These theories are interpreted as specifying that the outcome of individuals acting independently, without the intervention of any central authority, is just, provided that those who fare ill for reasons that the theories deem to be arbitrary. An example of this is because they have fewer talents than others and receive compensation from those who fare well. This book includes theories such as Rawls's justice as fairness, Dworkin's equality of resources, what may loosely be called Steiner-Vallentyne common ownership theories, and Nozick's entitlements theory. The book considers the extent, if any, to which the theories discussed, can accommodate both liberty and equality. It concludes that any such accommodation is problematic, but that if it is to be found it will be found among the common ownership theories" -- Provided by publisher.
   1. Distributive justice. I. Title.
   HB523.A445 2014
   340'.115--dc23
                  2013031222

ISBN: 978-0-415-85911-0 (hbk)
ISBN: 978-0-415-85910-3 (pbk)
ISBN: 978-1-315-81744-6 (ebk)

Typeset in Bembo
by Taylor & Francis Books

Printed and Bound in the United States of America by
Edwards Brothers Malloy

To Freddie, Daisy, Sebastian, and Philippa

CONTENTS

PREFACE

This is a book on political philosophy, though one that draws on economic theory. Its subject matter has been extensively explored by philosophers and, to a lesser extent, economists, but on the whole their two approaches have been distinct. Philosophers claim, with some reason, that economists force philosophical questions into formal frameworks that lose many of the nuances of the problem. Economists, on the other hand, claim that the work of philosophers is frequently too vague and informal to stand critical scrutiny. The book seeks to apply the logic of economic theory to the subject matter of political philosophy, but without (other than in an appendix) employing any mathematical apparatus. Although the book suggest various extensions to existing theories of justice, for example, in the introduction of a principle of free association and in the proposal for restrictions on re-gifting, its main aim is to present a critical appraisal of these theories in a unified framework.

Political philosophy, perhaps more than any other branch of philosophy, has much to say about people. Thus a large number of personal pronouns are unavoidable, or only avoidable by clumsy circumlocutions. (Rawls's *A Theory of Justice* uses 'he/him/his' over 1400 times.) To keep the phrasing simple, the masculine version is used throughout the book, but this is to be interpreted in an inclusive manner.

I am grateful to Scarlett Baron, Isabella Muzio, Amartya Sen, John Shand, and Polly Dyne Steel for their many helpful clarifications and suggestions, and I am particularly indebted to Hillel Steiner for a number of detailed comments. (All of the above are, of course, entirely responsible for any remaining errors.)

Two organizational points may be noted. The first is that all references are given in the endnotes, but if two or more quotations from the same page (or pages that are separated by at most one page) of a work are referred to in a single paragraph an endnote is provided only for the last such quotation. The second is that references to classical texts give both the book-part-section (or equivalent) location and the page number in a modern edition: thus 'Hume (1739/2000), 2.3.3, page 267' refers to Book 2, Part 3, Section 3 of *A Treatise of Human Nature*, and to page 267 of the specified 2000 edition.

MA

1

INTRODUCTION

This book presents a critical appraisal of the main theories of distributive justice, that is, theories that seek to specify what is meant by a just distribution of goods among members of society. It does so in a framework in which all liberal theories of justice are seen as expressions of laissez-faire with compensations for factors that they consider to be morally arbitrary. More specifically, such theories are interpreted as specifying that the outcome of individuals acting independently, without the intervention of any central authority, is just, provided that those who fare ill for reasons that the theories deem to be arbitrary, for example, because they have fewer talents than others, receive compensation from those who fare well.

A simple world

The simple world comprises a number of individuals and three commodities: a natural resource, called land; a consumption good, called food; and individuals' labour. There is a given amount of land, which is held by individuals, but no stock of food: food may be created from land and labour. An individual is characterized by his preferences between food and leisure (leisure being the obverse of labour); by his ability, or productivity in transforming land and labour into food; and by his holding of land.

A distribution is defined by each individual's consumption of food (or equivalently, his income), his expenditure of labour (or enjoyment of leisure), and his holding of land. An institution under which this may be achieved is a system of taxes and subsidies on income, and reallocation of holdings in land: these may range from pure laissez-faire at one end of the spectrum to 100 per cent taxes on income and complete appropriation of land at the other. A theory of justice specifies which institutions, or, equivalently, which distributions, are considered to be just. (It is assumed, for the time being, that there is a one-to-one correspondence between institutions and distributions.)

Liberal theories of justice consider the process, or outcome, of individuals' free actions to be just except insofar as this depends on factors, in the form of personal characteristics, which are considered to be morally arbitrary. In the present context these factors may be individuals' preferences, their abilities, and their holdings of land. We may, then, categorize such theories according to which of these factors each theory deems to be morally arbitrary.

Equality has various interpretations in this simple world: these correspond to the theories discussed below. Liberty has two aspects: self-ownership, that is, rights to one's body, one's labour, and the fruits thereof; and resource-ownership, that is, rights to own external resources and the produce of these. Theories that fail to maintain self-ownership may be divided into those that recognize personal responsibility, in that the extent of the incursions they make are independent of how people exercise these (for example, in being industrious or lazy), and those that do not.

In a liberal context there is (as is justified later) no basis for comparing one individual's wellbeing with another's, so that theories of justice which require such comparisons cannot be accommodated. Accordingly, the theories of utilitarianism, which defines a distribution to be just if it maximizes the sum of each individual's wellbeing, and of equality of welfare, which defines a distribution to be just if each individual has the same level of wellbeing, are not considered.

Four theories of justice are addressed: Rawlsian egalitarianism, or justice as fairness; Dworkinian egalitarianism, or equality of resources; Steiner-Vallentyne libertarianism, or common ownership; and Nozickian libertarianism, or entitlements. These names are used simply as labels: they do not imply sole authorship (particularly so in the case of the third). In each of these theories a just distribution may be interpreted as being that which would result from laissez-faire adjusted for various personal characteristics that are considered to be morally arbitrary. The following specification of the theories sets out, for each theory: its definition of justice; the personal characteristics that it considers to be arbitrary and therefore makes adjustments for; the nature of the institution under which this may be achieved; the justification of any inequalities which it accepts; and the extent to which it is consistent with liberty.

Justice as fairness defines a distribution to be just if it maximizes the food that the individual with the least food receives (this is the maximin outcome in terms of food, which is the sole primary good). It adjusts for preferences, ability, and land holdings. It is achieved by taxes and subsidies on income (that is, on the consumption of food). Inequalities in income, subject to the maximin requirement, are accepted because of the benefit they bring to the individual with the least income; all inequalities in leisure are accepted. Rights to neither self-ownership nor resource-ownership are maintained, and responsibility is not recognized.

Equality of resources defines a distribution to be just if everyone has the same effective resources, that is, if for some given amount of work each person could obtain the same amount of food. It adjusts for ability and land holdings, but not for preferences. It is achieved by taxes and subsidies on income. Inequalities in both food and leisure are accepted because they arise solely from choices made by individuals who have the same options. Rights to neither self-ownership nor resource-ownership are maintained, but responsibility is recognized.

Common ownership theories define a distribution to be just if each person initially has the same amount of land and all transactions between individuals are voluntary. It adjusts for land holdings, but not for preferences or abilities. It is achieved by a reallocation of holdings of land. Inequalities in both food and leisure are accepted because these arise solely from people having different preferences or abilities. Rights to self-ownership are maintained but rights to resource-ownership are not.

An entitlements theory defines a distribution to be just if the distribution of land is historically justified, that is if it arose from the appropriation by individuals of previously unowned land and voluntary transfers between individuals, and all other transactions between individuals are voluntary. It makes no adjustments (other than corrections for any improper acquisitions or transfers) and thus requires no imposed institution to achieve it. All inequalities are accepted. Rights to both self-ownership and resource-ownership are maintained.

As is apparent from these descriptions, the first two theories emphasize outcomes while the second two emphasize institutions. These four theories form a hierarchy, or decreasing progression, in terms of the personal characteristics that they consider to be morally arbitrary, and thus for which adjustments are made. The first theory adjusts for preferences, ability, and land holdings; the second only for ability and land holdings; the third only for land holdings; and the fourth for none of these (other than the corrections noted above). The four theories form a corresponding hierarchy, or increasing progression, in terms of the liberties (self-ownership, with or without personal responsibility, and resource-ownership) that they maintain: the first maintains neither, and does not recognize responsibility; the second maintains neither, but does recognize responsibility; the third maintains self-ownership but not resource-ownership; and the fourth maintains both self-ownership and resource-ownership. These corresponding hierarchies are illustrated schematically in Table 1.1 below.

The world portrayed above and the concepts developed in it are deliberately simple. The remainder of this book develops the four theories of justice which have been described in a more complex world. It demonstrates that they also form a third hierarchy in terms of equality (of outcome), with Rawls's justice as fairness as the most egalitarian, followed by Dworkin's equality of resources, then common

TABLE 1.1 A taxonomy

Theory	Arbitrary factors	Liberties maintained
Rawls	Preferences-Ability – Land	–
Dworkin	Ability – Land	Responsibility
Steiner-Vallentyne	Land	Responsibility – Self-ownership
Nozick	–	Responsibility – Self-ownership – Resource-ownership

ownership in the Steiner-Vallentyne vein, and finally Nozick's entitlements theory as the least egalitarian.

Background

The 1970s may have been described as 'the decade that style/taste forgot',[1] but it was also the decade that witnessed the awakening of political philosophy from its long post-utilitarian slumbers with the publication of John Rawls's *A Theory of Justice* in 1971 and Robert Nozick's *Anarchy, State, and Utopia* in 1974. As Meadowcroft notes, 'Rawls's *TJ* and Nozick's *ASU* provide two of the most important contributions to contemporary debates about justice';[2] they 'have framed the contemporary debate about the nature of justice by representing the two fundamental opposing views of what constitutes justice in the distribution of income and wealth'.[3]

The two views are 'fundamentally opposing' in a number of ways. In essence, Rawls emphasizes equality while Nozick emphasizes liberty. Rawls's justice as fairness approach argues that resources 'are to be distributed equally unless an unequal distribution … is to everyone's advantage'.[4] In contrast, Nozick's entitlements approach argues that 'individuals have rights, and there are things no person or group may do to them (without violating their rights)'.[5] The two approaches are also characterized by fundamentally different views of the nature of society. For Rawls, 'society is interpreted as a cooperative venture for mutual advantage',[6] whereas Nozick sees 'individuals in something sufficiently similar to Locke's state of nature'.[7] In Rawls's view cooperation arises through an (implicit) contract; in Nozick's it arises without any agreement, through an invisible hand. Rawls's is a top-down macro approach, Nozick's a bottom-up micro one.

The two treatments differ in style as well as in substance. *A Theory of Justice* is written in a careful, qualified, and at times prolix, manner. As Mandle notes, 'Elster is not alone in thinking that the argument in *A Theory of Justice* "is notoriously elliptical or worse"'.[8] *Anarchy, State, and Utopia*, on the other hand, is written in a manner that has been described by Wolff as 'self-consciously "flashy" and deliberatively provocative',[9] and by Williams as being 'of a very highly theoretical character; indeed its theories themselves have a tendency to pursue the virtues of formal elegance rather than of concrete realism, as witnessed by the presence of much economic theory'.[10]

Rawls developed the position set out in *A Theory of Justice* in a number of later works, most notably in *Political Liberalism*. However, these developments are primarily concerned with justice in its wider, political sense, rather than in its narrower, distributive sense. In particular, they seek to remove an inconsistency in the argument that the concept of justice as fairness is self-sustaining. Rawls states in *Political Liberalism* that 'all differences are consequences of removing that inconsistency', and that otherwise 'these lectures take the structure and content of *Theory* to remain substantially the same'.[11] Thus the analytical core of *A Theory of Justice* is retained with only a change in emphasis. Nozick, in contrast, did not return to the arguments of *Anarchy, State, and Utopia*, other than to make some brief qualifying observations on inheritance in *The Examined Life*.[12]

Rawls's theory has been developed by other writers in a number of directions. The most significant of these is Dworkin's equality of resources theory, set out in his *Philosophy & Public Affairs* article 'What is equality? Part 2'. The essence of this development is its introduction into Rawls's framework of an element of personal responsibility, accepting inequalities if these arise from people's actions for which they are responsible. Nozick's theory has also been developed in diverse ways. These have their origins in the nineteenth-century writings of Léon Walras, Henry George, and others; a number of the more prominent of their modern incarnations are collected in Vallentyne and Steiner's *Left Libertarianism and Its Critics*. What all these contributions have in common is a retention of Nozick's rights of self-ownership but a rejection of his rights to ownership of the external world.

These two sets of developments each move towards some accommodation between the apparently 'fundamentally opposing' views of Rawls and Nozick. However, achieving any such accommodation is no simple task, as MacIntyre emphasizes:

> Rawls makes primary what is in effect a principle of equality with respect to needs … Nozick makes primary what is a principle of equality with respect to entitlements. … How can a claim that gives priority to equality of needs be rationally weighed against one which gives priority to entitlements?[13]

The view that liberal theories of distributive justice are expressions of laissez-faire with compensation for arbitrary factors may be seen as imposing some structure on the dominant (but amorphous) class of theories characterized by Arneson as follows:

> The concern of distributive justice is to compensate individuals for misfortune. Some people are blessed with good luck, some are cursed with bad luck, and it is the responsibility of society – all of us regarded collectively – to alter the distribution of goods and evils that arises from the jumble of lotteries that constitutes human life as we know it. … Distributive justice stipulates that the lucky should transfer some or all of their gains due to luck to the unlucky.[14]

This position, which 'can be traced to the work of John Rawls', is what Anderson (who criticizes it robustly) calls 'luck egalitarianism'; as Anderson makes clear, 'recent egalitarian writing has come to be dominated'[15] by it.

Four limitations

The theories of justice considered in this book are all liberal, in that they do not presuppose any particular conception of the good. They subscribe to what Sandel (who rejects this position) calls deontological liberalism:

'Deontological liberalism' is above all a theory about justice, and in particular about the primacy of justice among moral and political ideals. Its core thesis can be stated as follows: society, being composed of a plurality of persons, each with his own aims, interests, and conceptions of the good, is best arranged when it is governed by principles that do not *themselves* presuppose any particular conception of the good; what justifies these regulative principles above all is not that they ... promote the good, but rather that they conform to the concept of *right*, a moral category given prior to the good and independent of it. This is the liberalism of Kant and of much contemporary moral and political philosophy.[16]

Although the theories discussed are all liberal in this sense their proponents do not all agree that competing theories are liberal. For example, Rawls describes Nozick's position as being 'an impoverished form of liberalism, indeed not liberalism',[17] while Cohen (from a Marxist, and thus far from a Nozickian, perspective) states that 'Rawls and Dworkin ... are not liberals'.[18] There is an unfortunate etymological similarity between the words 'liberal' and 'liberty' that may seem to imply that the former necessarily implies the latter. In the senses defined above that is not the case: a theory that is liberal in the deontological sense may entail none or any or all of the liberties specified above. As attention is restricted to theories that are liberal in the deontological sense, theories such as communitarianism (proposed by Sandel as an alternative to deontological liberalism) and Marxism are not discussed.

A second limitation is that the discussion is restricted to what might be called the narrow question of distributive justice as opposed to the wider one of political justice. That is, it concentrates on the distribution of goods to individuals, and institutions that might achieve this, rather than on higher-level principles, such as democracy, in which these may be situated. Rawls devotes a substantial part of *A Theory of Justice*, and even more of *Political Liberalism*, to ideal institutions and political legitimacy; and Nozick similarly devotes much of *Anarchy, State, and Utopia* to minimal states that result from voluntary association. These aspects are not discussed.

A third limitation is that it is assumed that there is a given fixed population, each member of which is, to employ Locke's definition, 'a thinking intelligent being, that has reason and reflection'.[19] Thus there is no discussion of children or the mentally incapable, of inter-generational justice (other than as regards gifts and bequests), or of justice among nations. Also, non-natural persons, such as corporations, are ignored: as such persons are the creatures of the state the state may legitimately attach whatever conditions it sees fit to their activities.

A final, and perhaps the most important, limitation is that no consideration is given to the financing of institutions, such as the rule of law, under which just distributions are to be implemented. Rawls seeks to avoid this by distinguishing between different branches of the state, some of which in effect provide public goods, such as the rule of law, while others 'preserve an approximate justice in distributive shares by means of taxation and the necessary adjustments in the rights of property'.[20] Similarly, Nozick envisages protective associations, financed by voluntary contributions, which will guarantee individuals' entitlements. However, the separation of distributive justice from the public goods element of the framework in which this is to apply is not entirely satisfactory.

It should be emphasized that making these limitations does not imply that there is little of interest in communitarianism or Marxism, in the wider political aspects of justice, in inter-generational justice or justice among nations, or in public goods. It simply delineates the boundaries of the enquiry.

Some preliminaries

Four preliminary matters that require some attention are the role of rationality, the nature of utility, uncertainty, and the Pareto principle.

Rationality

Theories of justice that respect individual autonomy necessarily involve individual choices, and thus some notion of rational choice. Indeed, in Rawls's view 'the theory of justice is a part, perhaps *the most significant part*, of the theory of rational choice'.[21] Rational choice theory assumes no conception of the good: choice is not deemed to be rational or irrational because it accords with or does not accord with some imposed conception. Also, it does not assume self-interest: both altruistic and self-interested choices may be rational or irrational. The theory simply says that choice is rational if it is consistent in some sense. A basic condition for my choice to be rational, or consistent, is the axiom of revealed preference. This states that if I ever choose an option X when another option Y is available then whenever I choose Y and X is available I also choose X. An analogy is that if one horse wins, either outright or in a dead-heat, a race in which a second horse runs then the second horse will not win outright any race in which the first runs.

My preferences specify, for any two options, say X and Y, whether I consider X to be at least as good as Y, or Y to be at least as good as X. This allows for the possibility of both applying: if this is the case then I consider the two options to be indifferent. And if X is at least as good as Y but the two are not indifferent then I consider X to be better than Y, or, more simply, I prefer X to Y. Preferences are a rationalization of choices: if I choose X over Y (that is choose X alone when Y is available) then I consider X to be better than Y, and so forth. Equivalently, choices are an expression of preferences: if I prefer X to Y then I choose X over Y.

Preferences may also be considered rational or irrational. Three basic conditions for my preferences to be rational are: that they are reflexive, in that each option is at least as good as itself; that they are complete, in that given any two options I either prefer one to the other or am indifferent between the two; and that they are transitive, in that if I prefer one option to a second and the second to a third then I prefer the first to the third (and similarly for indifference). It may readily be shown[22] that if my preferences are rational then so are my choices, and that if my choices are rational then so are my preferences.

This position formalizes what Griffin has called the taste model of desire and value, in contrast with the perception model: 'the perception model gives priority to value: desired because valuable', whereas 'the taste model reverses the priority: valuable because desired'.[23] Each model makes a separation between feeling or passion on the one hand and reason or judgement on the other. On the perception model I form a (derivative) preference between two options only after having, somehow, decided on their value; on the taste model I have preferences for one option over another simply because I want it more. The taste model is encapsulated in Hume's famous dictum that 'reason is and ought only to be the slave of the passions'. Passions, in this view are primitive: 'a passion can never, in any sense, be called unreasonable'; thus 'it is not contrary to reason to prefer the destruction of the whole world to the scratching of my finger; it is not contrary to reason for me to chuse my total ruin to prevent the least uneasiness of an *Indian*'.[24] As Griffin (who rejects the taste model) notes, 'the taste model is widespread in philosophy'.[25]

As (on the taste model) my preferences are primitive they are clearly *my* preferences: as regards my preferences I am sovereign. As Mill expresses it in his classical statement of liberalism, 'in the part [of someone's conduct] which merely concerns himself, his independence is, of right, absolute', so that 'over himself, over his own body and mind, the individual is sovereign'.[26] In this view, I am responsible for my preferences. In the context of distributive justice I am characterized by my preferences, and other external attributes: there is no higher mental part of me that can determine my preferences. They are, to repeat, primitive.

To say that I am responsible for my preferences is not to say that external events do not shape them. If I am brought up as a Christian in the West I may have a different outlook on life, and different preferences, than I would if I were brought up as a Buddhist in the East. Rather, it is to say that I am not to be favoured or compensated for having or not having a Christian, or Buddhist, outlook on life and preferences. As Scanlon puts it, 'the choice of religion (or no religion) is entirely up to each person, and the amount of utility resulting from this choice is specifically not an object of public policy',[27] a position which Arneson echoes more forcefully: 'we would regard it as absurd to insist upon compensation in the name of distributive equality for having been raised fundamentalist Protestant rather than atheist or Catholic (a matter that of course does not lie within the individual's power to control)'.[28]

Utility

Many theories of justice make use of the concept of wellbeing, or welfare, or utility. Utility in the sense used here is a numerical representation of preference, and nothing else: if I prefer one option to a second then I assign a higher utility to the first than to the second. It may readily be shown[29] that if my preferences are rational then (at least if I have only a finite number of options) I can consistently assign utilities in this way, and if I can assign utilities then my preferences are rational. Then, as preference is equivalent to choice, the following three statements are equivalent: (1) I choose X over Y; (2) I prefer X to Y; and (3) I assign a higher utility to X than to Y. The relevance of this equivalence is that as choices are, in principle, observable, then so are utility rankings: my assigning a higher utility to X than to Y is, in principle, empirically observable. However, utility is simply the numerical representation of something real: I do not choose X (over Y) because it gives me more utility; rather, I assign a higher utility to X because I choose it.

The fact that utility rankings are, in principle, observable, does not imply that differences in utility are observable (other than in being positive or negative) or have any meaning. If I rank three options in order of decreasing preference X, Y, and Z then I may assign a utility of 2 to X, 1 to Y, and 0 to Z; or I may assign a utility of 100 to X, 99 to Y, and 1 to Z. These assignments are equivalent: they convey precisely the same information. Thus statements such as 'I prefer X to Y more than I prefer Y to Z' have no meaning. This is to say that utility is ordinal rather than cardinal.

Further, the fact that my utility rankings are, in principle, observable and that yours are observable does not imply that our utilities may be compared. You may rank the three options in the above example in the same way that I do, which is to say that we have identical preferences, but you may assign utilities in the first way and I may assign them in the second. It would be absurd to claim that I am better off than you just because I assign utilities in a different way to you. Indeed, there is no conceptual experiment that would determine whether or not I was better off than you. Suppose that you are rich but have only one leg, and I am poor but have both my legs. I would prefer to be in your shoes (or shoe) than in mine, and you would prefer to be in my shoes than in yours. Which of us is the worse off? I claim that I am worse off than you, and you claim that you are worse off than me. Who is to adjudicate? Any adjudication must involve an arbitrary, and, in a liberal context, unwarranted, specification of the good.

Any interpersonal comparisons of utility necessarily involve such value judgements. As Scanlon (who supports interpersonal comparisons) accepts, 'within contemporary political philosophy … interpersonal comparisons present a problem insofar as it is assumed that the judgements of relative well-being on which social policy decisions, or claims of justice, are based should not reflect value judgements'.[30] And Hammond, who also supports interpersonal comparisons, accepts that such comparisons 'really do require that an individual's utility be the ethical utility or worth of that individual to the society'.[31] If we are not prepared to take a position on someone's worth to society then we cannot engage in interpersonal utility comparisons. It is in the light of this that Arrow notes that 'it requires a definite value judgement not derivable from individual sensations to make the utilities of different individuals dimensionally compatible and a still further value judgement to aggregate them', and accordingly concludes that 'interpersonal comparison of utilities has no meaning and, in fact, … there is no meaning relevant to welfare comparisons in the measurability of individual utility'.[32]

It is worth noting in passing that even Bentham, the founder of utilitarianism, in which the interpersonal comparability of utility is of the essence, had his qualms: it is 'in vain to talk of adding quantities which after the addition will continue distinct as they were before, one man's happiness will never be another man's happiness; … you might as well pretend to add 20 apples to 20 pears'.[33]

In summary, the position on utility adopted in what follows is that it is not meaningful to compare one person's utility with another's. However, this is not to claim that interpersonal comparisons have no meaning in other contexts, such as where there is some specified conception of the good.

Uncertainty

The discussion of rational choice above assumed that there was no uncertainty. It is also necessary to consider choice under uncertainty, and thus probability, particularly for the discussion of Rawls's justice as fairness theory. As Rawls observes, 'it may be surprising that the meaning of probability should arise as a problem in moral philosophy, especially in the theory of justice'; however, it is 'the inevitable consequence of the contract doctrine which conceives of moral philosophy as part of the theory of rational choice'.[34]

Because of its particular relevance to Rawls's theory, the present discussion, although of general applicability, is expressed in the context of that theory. In this, there is a set of possible distributions of some good or goods, referred to here for simplicity of exposition as income. For example, one distribution may allocate an income of 100 to nurses, 300 to bankers, and so forth; and another may allocate an income of 200 to each. I have to choose a distribution not knowing what position in it I will occupy, that is, not knowing whether I will be a nurse or a banker.

Just as choosing rationally under certainty means choosing according to the revealed preference axiom, choosing rationally under uncertainty means choosing according to corresponding axioms. Essentially, these are (a) an independence axiom, which requires that my choice between two uncertain prospects be independent of the aspects that they share, and (b) a continuity axiom, which requires that my preferences over prospects vary continuously as the prospects change. These axioms are set out formally by Savage,[35] and more accessibly by Kreps and by Allingham.[36] For expository purposes, it is useful to proceed in two stages: that in which the probabilities of my occupying the various positions, that is, of being a nurse or a banker, and so forth, are supposed to be given; and that in which they are not.

In the first case the axioms imply that I evaluate a distribution by assigning a utility to each position in that distribution and computing my expected utility for the distribution. This expected utility is obtained by multiplying the given probability associated with each income by the utility assigned to it and adding the resulting numbers. For example, if the probabilities of my having an income of 100 and 200 are ⅓ and ⅔ and I have assigned utilities of 3 and 6 to these two levels respectively then my expected utility is 5. Having done this for all feasible distributions I choose the one with the highest expected utility. If there are only a finite number of distributions, or under some plausible technical assumptions even if there are not, there will always be some, not necessarily unique, distribution with the highest expected utility.

I may assign utility numbers in various ways: for example, I might without any change in my preferences assign 7 and 13, rather than 3 and 6, to the two incomes. However, all the ways in which I may assign utilities are affine transformations of one another: that is, I may change my utilities by multiplying each by the same positive number and by adding the same number to each, but not otherwise. My being able to assign utilities, and do so in this manner, is not an arbitrary assumption: it is a direct implication of the axioms of rationality. (The restriction on the ways in which I may assign utility may appear to suggest that utility is cardinal. However, this cardinality reflects only my attitude to risk, not the strength of my preference for a higher income. Further, even if my utility were cardinal this would not imply that it could meaningfully be compared with yours.)

In the second case, that in which the probabilities of my occupying the various positions are not given, the axioms imply that I assign my own probabilities and then proceed as if these were given. Assigning probabilities is analogous to assigning utilities. The latter is a numerical representation of preferences: it involves assigning numbers to positions such that more preferred positions have higher numbers. The former is a numerical representation of beliefs: it involves assigning numbers to positions such that more probable positions have higher numbers. If I believe that I am more likely to be a banker than a nurse then I assign a higher number to the former than to the latter. The only restriction on the numbers assigned is that, as they are to be construed as probabilities, they must all be non-negative and their sum must be 1. Again, my being able to assign probabilities, and do so in this manner, is not an arbitrary assumption: it is a direct implication of the axioms of rationality. In the context of choice under uncertainty probabilities are simply numerical representations of degrees of belief, and thus subjective; in some cases, such as rolling dice, there may be more evidence on which to base this belief than in others, such as forecasting the weather, but in each case probabilities are subjective.

A problem, known as the state dependency problem, would arise if utilities depended on the state of the world. In Rawls's context this would be the case if I assigned utilities of, say, 3 and 6 to two income levels in one distribution, and of 3 and 7 to the same income levels in another. However, this problem does not arise if (as Rawls assumes) I only care about my own income level.

The Pareto principle

Accepting that utilities cannot be compared does not mean that no comparisons can be made between distributions. If everyone prefers one distribution to a second then we may judge the former to be better than the latter without employing any interpersonal comparisons. This is the (weak) Pareto criterion: the first distribution is weakly Pareto superior to the second. A distribution is weakly Pareto efficient if there is no weakly Pareto superior distribution. If no one prefers the second distribution and at least one person prefers the first then the first is Pareto superior in the standard, or strong, sense. And a distribution is strongly Pareto efficient if there is no strongly Pareto superior distribution. More simply, it is Pareto efficient if it is not possible to make one person better off without making another worse off. If a distribution is strongly Pareto efficient then it is weakly Pareto efficient, but not conversely. However, in many, but not all, contexts, the two are equivalent. If I prefer the first distribution and everyone else is indifferent between the two it may well be that if a small amount of some good is taken from me, sufficiently small that I still prefer the first distribution, and redistributed to everyone else in equal shares then everyone will prefer the first distribution to the second.

The Pareto criterion specifies only a partial, not a complete, ordering of distributions, so that there will typically be many Pareto efficient distributions. Pareto efficiency is not sufficient for justice, but it is widely accepted to be a necessary condition. As Rawls, who refers to the Pareto principle as 'the principle of efficiency',[37] notes,

> There are ... many efficient arrangements of the basic structure. Each of these specifies a division of advantages from social cooperation. The problem is to choose between them, to find a conception of justice that singles out one of these efficient distributions as also just. If we succeed in this, we shall have gone *beyond* mere efficiency *yet in a way compatible with it*. ... The principle of efficiency cannot serve *alone* as a conception of justice. Therefore it must be *supplemented* in some way.[38]

An outline

Kymlicka notes that 'it is generally accepted that the recent rebirth of normative political philosophy began with the publication of John Rawls's *A Theory of Justice*', a book which sets out a theory that 'dominates contemporary debates, not because everyone accepts it, but because alternative views are often presented as responses to it'.[39] This theory is discussed in Chapter 2. The most significant development of Rawls's theory is Dworkin's equality of resources theory, which allows more scope for responsibility than does Rawls's theory; this forms the subject matter of Chapter 3. The most radical alternative to Rawls's and Dworkin's theories is Nozick's entitlements theory, radical in that it does not look at patterns of distribution, but asks how these have come about; this is presented in Chapter 4. And the most wide-ranging revisions of Nozick's theory are those in the Steiner-Vallentyne common ownership vein, which retain Nozick's requirement of self-ownership but replace his requirement of resource-ownership with some form of common ownership; these theories are discussed in Chapter 5.

As is apparent, the order in which these theories are discussed differs from that of the decreasing progression in terms of the personal characteristics that they consider to be morally arbitrary: specifically, the discussion of entitlements precedes that of common ownership. The reason for this is that common ownership theories follow temporally, and draw on, Nozick's entitlements theory.

The final chapter discusses the problems of choosing between competing theories of justice, and considers whether any theory can accommodate both liberty and equality.

Notes

 1 Hunt (1998), page 1.
 2 Meadowcroft (2011), page 194.
 3 Meadowcroft (2011), pages 168–69.
 4 Rawls (1999a), page 24.
 5 Nozick (1974), page ix.
 6 Rawls (1999a), pages 72–73.
 7 Nozick (1974), page 9.
 8 Mandle (2009), pages 17–18.
 9 Wolff (1991), page 1.
10 Williams (1982), page 35.
11 Rawls (2005), page xvi.
12 Nozick (1989), pages 30–32.
13 MacIntyre (2007), pages 248–49.
14 Arneson (2008), page 80.
15 Anderson (1999), pages 288–90.
16 Sandel (1998), page 1.
17 Rawls (2005), page lviii.
18 Cohen (1986), pages 114–15.
19 Locke (1690/2008), 2.27.9, page 208.
20 Rawls (1999a), page 245.
21 Rawls (1999a), page 15, emphasis added.
22 Allingham (1999), chapter 1, for example.
23 Griffin (1991), page 45.
24 Hume (1739/2000), 2.3.3, page 267.
25 Griffin (1991), page 45.
26 Mill (1865), page 6.
27 Scanlon (1986), page 117.
28 Arneson (1989), page 80.
29 Allingham (1999), chapter 1, for example.
30 Scanlon (1991), page 17.
31 Hammond (1991), page 237.
32 Arrow (2012), pages 9–11.
33 Unpublished manuscript quoted by Halévy (1904), page 481.
34 Rawls (1999a), page 149.
35 Savage (1954), sections 2.4–2.7, 3.2–3.3, 5.2, 5.4.
36 Kreps (1988), chapter 9, and Allingham (2002), chapter 3.
37 Rawls (1999a), page 56.
38 Rawls (1999a), pages 61–62, emphasis added.
39 Kymlicka (2002), page 10.

2

JUSTICE AS FAIRNESS

In the framework in which justice is interpreted as laissez-faire with compensation for morally arbitrary factors, justice as fairness, as developed by Rawls,[1] treats all personal attributes as being morally arbitrary, and thus defines justice as requiring equality, unless any departure from this benefits everyone. This view is summarized in Rawls's 'general conception of justice', which is that 'all social values – liberty and opportunity, income and wealth, and the social bases of self-respect – are to be distributed equally unless an unequal distribution of any, or all, of these values is to everyone's advantage': injustice 'is simply inequalities that are not to the benefit of all'.[2]

Two principles

Rawls's interpretation is made more precise in his two principles of justice. He proposes a number of formulations of these; the final formulation is that of *Political Liberalism*:

   a. Each person has an equal claim to a fully adequate scheme of equal basic rights and liberties, which scheme is compatible with the same scheme for all; and in this scheme the equal political liberties, and only those liberties, are to be guaranteed their fair value.
   b. Social and economic inequalities are to satisfy two conditions: first, they are to be attached to positions and offices open to all under conditions of fair equality of opportunity; and second, they are to be to the greatest benefit of the least advantaged members of society.[3]

These principles are lexically ordered: the first principle has priority over the second; and in the second principle the first part has priority over the second part. For the specific question of distributive justice, as opposed to the wider question of political justice, it is the final stone in the edifice that is crucial. This is the difference principle, that inequalities 'are to be adjusted so that, whatever the level of those inequalities, whether great or small, they are to the greatest benefit of the least advantaged members of society'.[4]

A social contract

Rawls justifies his two principles of justice by a social contract argument. For Rawls, a just state of affairs is a state on which people would agree in an original state of nature. Rawls seeks 'to generalize and carry to a higher order of abstraction the traditional theory of the social contract as represented by Locke, Rousseau, and Kant', and to do so in a way 'that it is no longer open to the more obvious objections often thought fatal to it'.[5]

The most evident of these obvious objections is that there never was any such contract, or any identifiable original state of nature in which it might have been made. Rawls avoids this objection by making it clear that his original position, and thus contract, is hypothetical, not historical:

> The original position of equality corresponds to the state of nature in the traditional theory of the social contract. This original position is not, of course, thought of as an actual historical state of affairs, much less as a primitive condition of culture. It is understood as a purely hypothetical situation characterized so as to lead to a certain conception of justice.[6]

This, however, does not avoid a second objection, that any hypothetical agreement is irrelevant from a moral point of view. As Nozick observes, 'tacit consent [or agreement] isn't worth the paper it's not written on'.[7] Or as Dworkin sees it, Rawls's contract 'is hypothetical, and hypothetical contracts do not supply an independent argument for the fairness of enforcing their terms'; indeed, 'a hypothetical agreement is not simply a pale form of an actual contract; it is no contract at all'.[8] Dworkin gives as an example of a hypothetical agreement the case of someone who would have accepted $100 for a painting that he owned on Monday, but who discovers on Tuesday that it is worth more than that. The fact that he would, though did not, agree to sell the painting for $100 on Monday cannot compel him to sell it for $100 on Wednesday.

An alternative interpretation of the social contract that is neither historical nor hypothetical is that it is a thought-experiment for exploring the implications of an assumption of moral equality as embodied in the original position. This interpretation is implicit in Rawls's suggestion that 'one way to look at the idea of the original position, therefore, is to see it as an expository device which sums up the meaning of these conditions [for justice] and helps us to extract their consequences'.[9] But under whatever interpretation, the original position has its problems: as Dworkin puts it, 'the device of an original position … cannot plausibly be taken as the starting point for political philosophy'.[10]

If the social contract is interpreted as a thought-experiment for exploring the implications of moral equality in the original position, then that position must clearly be one of moral equality. To give effect to this Rawls assumes that the parties to the contract 'are situated behind a veil of ignorance' where they do not know anything about themselves or their situations, and accordingly are equal. The concept of the veil of ignorance, which Rawls borrows from Harsanyi,[11] is implicit in the Kantian categorical imperative, or in Sidgwick's acknowledgement that 'if I judge any action to be right for myself, I implicitly judge it to be right for anyone else whose nature and circumstances don't differ significantly from mine'.[12]

Rawls's veil of ignorance is a thick veil:

> No one knows his place in society, his class position or social status; nor does he know his fortune in the distribution of natural assets and abilities, his intelligence and strength, and the like. Nor, again, does anyone know his conception of the good, the particulars of his rational plan of life, or even the special features of his psychology such as his aversion to risk or liability to optimism or pessimism. More than this, I assume that the parties do not know the particular circumstances of their own society. That is, they do not know its economic or political situation, or the level of civilization and culture it has been able to achieve.[13]

The intention is that as the parties to the contract have no information about themselves they necessarily act impartially, and thus as justice as fairness requires. As no one knows his circumstances, no one can try to impose principles of justice that favour his particular condition. In this, there is a connection with Smith's view that a system is just if it meets the approval of an impartial spectator: 'the most vulgar education teaches us to act, upon all important occasions, with some sort of impartiality between ourselves and others'.[14] Although Rawls recognizes that 'there may be several problems with this [impartial spectator] definition', the essential point is that 'there is no conflict so far between this definition and justice as fairness'.[15] Nonetheless, the two approaches differ. The impartial spectator approach does not derive its principles of justice from any more basic assumptions; rather, it identifies the central features, such as impartiality and reflection, which characterize moral judgements. The contract view goes further: it seeks to provide a basis for the principles that underlie these features.

A conceptual problem with Rawls's thick veil of ignorance is that it is unclear that there is any sense of self left in the contractors when they are stripped of all the attributes that Rawls specifies. As Kymlicka notes, 'many critics have viewed this demand that people distance themselves from knowledge of their social background and individual desires as evidence of a bizarre theory of personal identity'.[16] In what sense can a contractor be 'a thinking intelligent being, that has reason and reflection' when there is nothing on which to reflect? However, the veil of ignorance is not concerned with personal identity. Rather, it is an intuitive test of fairness, as is that involved in the procedure for dividing a cake in which the person cutting the cake does not know which slice he will have. As Rawls emphasizes,

> One should not be misled, then, by the somewhat unusual conditions which characterize the original position. The idea here is simply to make vivid to ourselves the restrictions that it seems reasonable to impose on arguments for principles of justice, and therefore on these principles themselves. ... In this manner the veil of ignorance is arrived at in a natural way.[17]

The specification of any contract requires the specification of the contractors. Rawls does not suppose that the contractors are 'at one moment everyone who will live at some time; or, much less, as an assembly of everyone who could live at some time'; the contract 'is not a gathering of all actual or possible persons'. Because contractors choose from behind the veil of ignorance it is immaterial who they are. Accordingly, 'we can view the agreement in the original position from the standpoint of one person selected at random'.[18]

This device avoids all intertemporal problems, for 'whatever a person's temporal position, each is forced to choose for all'.[19] It may be that the contractors see themselves as 'heads of families and therefore have a desire to further the well-being of at least their more immediate descendants', or alternatively that they 'agree to principles subject to the constraint that they wish all preceding generations to have followed the very same principles'. Either way, 'the whole chain of generations can be tied together and principles agreed to that suitably take into account the interests of each'.[20]

The difference principle

Rawls argues that in the social contract formed behind a veil of ignorance the contractors will adopt his two principles of justice, and in particular the difference principle: that all inequalities 'are to be to the greatest benefit of the least advantaged members of society'.

Rawls identifies three possible levels of justice under the difference principle, which he illustrates in the case where there are two classes, the advantaged and the disadvantaged. The first possibility is that in which the disadvantaged cannot be made better off whatever change is made to the advantaged; this Rawls considers to be 'a perfectly just scheme'. The second is that in which if the advantaged were made worse off the disadvantaged would also be made worse off, but if the advantaged were made better off the disadvantaged would also be made better off; this case is 'just throughout, but not the best just arrangement'. The third is that in which if the advantaged were made worse off the disadvantaged would be made better off; this case is 'unjust'.[21]

Implicit in the difference principle is the recognition that the question of distribution is not zero-sum: it is not that of dividing a given cake. If it were then Rawls would have no reason to depart from the prescription of absolute equality.

Rather, the principle recognizes that the proportions in which the cake is to be distributed may affect the size of the cake. For example, inequalities may encourage people to work more; or they may 'act as incentives so that the economic process is more efficient, innovation proceeds at a faster pace';[22] or they may constitute 'a way to put resources in the hands of those who can make the best social use of them'.[23] Under each of these three mechanisms inequalities may make the cake larger. It is also possible that inequalities may make the cake smaller: for example, they may sap morale so that people put less effort into their work. However, such cases may be ignored, for if the cake becomes smaller then at least one person must have a smaller slice than he would have under an equal distribution, so that the equal distribution would be preferred.

It is central to Rawls's position that there be no trade-off between equality and the size of the cake. Suppose that if you and I divide a cake equally, we each have slices weighing 100 grams, but that other distributions, and corresponding sizes of cake, are possible. Then the distribution in which my and your slices each weigh 101 grams is preferred to that in which yours weighs 900 grams and mine 100. But Rawls's position also takes no account of any inequality other than at the bottom of the distribution. Thus the distribution in which your and my slices each weigh 101 grams and that of some third party weighs 900 grams is preferred to that in which everyone's slice weighs 100 grams, despite the marked inequality between us and the third party in the first distribution but not the second.

More formally, denote the level of wellbeing of the worst-off member of society in the distribution D by $W(D)$. Then the difference principle specifies that the distribution $D1$ is at least as just as the distribution $D2$ if $W(D1)$ is at least as great as $W(D2)$; this is equivalent to everyone in $D1$ being at least as well off as is the worst-off member of society in the distribution $D2$ in that distribution. Statements such as this do, problematically, require some comparisons of wellbeing: specifically, they require that the worst-off members of society can be identified, and that the wellbeing of those members of society can be compared. However, as will be seen, Rawls claims that this does not involve any interpersonal comparisons of utility.

The relation specified by the difference principle is clearly reflexive, that is, any distribution is at least as just as itself. This relation is also complete, that is, given any two distributions $D1$ and $D2$ either $D1$ is at least as just as $D2$, or $D2$ is at least as just as $D1$ (or both). This is because either $W(D1)$ is at least as great as $W(D2)$, or $W(D2)$ is at least as great as $W(D1)$ (or both). And finally, the relation is transitive, in that given any three distributions $D1$, $D2$, and $D3$, if $D1$ is at least as just as $D2$ and $D2$ is at least as just as $D3$ then $D1$ is at least as just as $D3$. This is because if $W(D1)$ is at least as great as $W(D2)$ and $W(D2)$ is at least as great as $W(D3)$ then $W(D1)$ must be at least as great as $W(D3)$. Given these three properties, reflexivity, completeness, and transitivity, there is (at least under some plausible technical assumptions) some, not necessarily unique, most just distribution. Then a distribution is just in an absolute sense if it is a most just distribution. Equivalently, the distribution $D1$ (in which the worst-off member of society is X) is just in an absolute sense if there is no feasible alternative distribution $D2$ such that $W(D2)$ is greater than $W(D1)$, that is, if there is no feasible alternative distribution in which everyone is better off than X is in the distribution $D1$. Note that the requirement is that everyone is better off, not just that X is. That is, the least advantaged functions as a definite description rather than a rigid designator: the purpose of the difference principle is to 'make the worst off (*whoever they may be* …) better off than the worst off (*whoever they may be*) under any alternative (practicable) scheme'.[24]

The distribution $D1$ is more just than the distribution $D2$ if it is at least as just as $D2$ but $D2$ is not at least as just as $D1$. Equivalently, $D1$ is more just than $D2$ if $W(D1)$ is greater than $W(D2)$. By way of comparison, the distribution $D1$ is superior to the distribution $D2$ in the weak Pareto sense if each member of society is better off in $D1$ than he is $D2$. But if each member of society is better off in $D1$ than he is $D2$ then the minimum level of wellbeing in $D1$ must be greater than that in $D2$, which is to say that $W(D1)$ is greater than $W(D2)$, so that $D1$ is more just than $D2$. Thus a weak Pareto improvement is always an improvement in justice. However the converse does not apply. Returning to the cake example, assume that in $D1$ we each have slices weighing 100 grams and in $D2$ your slice weighs 110 grams and my slice weighs 90; then $D1$ is more just than $D2$, but is not Pareto superior.

Rawls makes a similar connection between the difference principle and the Pareto principle (Rawls's 'principle of efficiency') in claiming that 'the difference principle is compatible with the principle of efficiency'.[25] However, this is not entirely clear, for earlier Rawls accepts that 'actually, in justice as fairness the principles of justice are prior to considerations of efficiency and therefore, roughly speaking, the interior [inefficient] points that represent just distributions will generally be preferred to efficient points which represent unjust distributions'.[26]

Rawls does not distinguish between the weak form of the Pareto principle and the standard form. In some instances Rawls intends the standard form, for example, when he specifies that 'a distribution of goods or a scheme of production is inefficient when there are ways of doing still better for *some* individuals without doing any worse for others',[27] or in stating that when his principle of efficiency is satisfied 'it is indeed impossible to make *any one* representative man better off without making another worse off'. In other instances he intends the weak form, for example, when he notes that 'if the principle is satisfied, *everyone* is benefited', and 'one obvious sense in which this is so is that *each man's* position is improved'.[28]

The distinction between the standard and the weak forms of the Pareto principle is relevant because the difference principle is not compatible with the standard form; that is, a standard Pareto improvement may not be an improvement in justice. Equivalently, even though a distribution is just it may be possible to make someone better off without making anyone worse off. Returning again to the cake example, assume that in the distribution $D1$ your slice weighs 200 grams and my slice weighs 100, while in the distribution $D2$ your slice weighs 300 grams and mine weighs 100. Then $D2$ is Pareto superior in the standard sense to $D1$, but it is not more just: $D1$ and $D2$ are equally just. The distribution $D1$ is just, but a move to $D2$ makes someone better off and no one worse off: it is a standard Pareto improvement but not an improvement in justice.

Although he does not explicitly address the distinction between weak and standard Pareto improvement, Rawls implicitly does so when proposing two simplifying assumptions. The first is that inequalities are 'chain-connected: that is, if an advantage has the effect of raising the expectations of the lowest position, it raises the expectations of all positions in between'. Note that this says nothing about the case where the least advantaged do not gain, so that it does not mean that all effects move together. The second assumption is that inequalities are 'close-knit: that is, it is impossible to raise or lower the expectation of any representative man without raising or lowering the expectation of every other representative man, especially that of the least advantaged'. If these assumptions do not hold then 'it is clearly conceivable, however likely or important in practice, that the least advantaged are not affected one way or the other by some changes in expectations of the best off although these changes benefit others'.[29]

To cover the cases where the close-knit and chain connection assumptions do not apply Rawls (following Sen[30]) proposes a more general principle:

> In a basic structure with n relevant representatives, first maximize the welfare of the worst off representative man; second, for equal welfare of the worst-off representative, maximize the welfare of the second worst-off representative man, and so on until the last case which is, for equal welfare of all the preceding n-1 representatives, maximize the welfare of the best-off representative man.[31]

It is not clear why Rawls introduces this principle, which he terms the lexical principle, since he claims that 'the general laws governing the institutions of the basic structure insure that cases requiring the lexical principle will not arise'; accordingly, he will 'always use the difference principle in the simpler form'.[32] Nonetheless, as the example above demonstrating that a standard Pareto improvement may not be an improvement in justice shows, such cases may well arise. And introducing the lexical principle is important because, as arguments analogous to those presented above readily demonstrate, the lexical difference principle is compatible with the standard form of the Pareto principle.

The least advantaged

Since the difference principle prescribes that inequalities 'are to be to the greatest benefit of the least advantaged members of society' it is necessary to consider who comprise the least advantaged. There are four aspects to this: what constitutes the members of society (or their representatives); what counts as being advantaged; how the advantages of one member are to be compared with those of another; and, more generally, the robustness of the concept of the least advantaged.

The members of society

It would seem natural in defining the least advantaged members of society to identify the least advantaged *individuals*, but Rawls does not do this. Instead, he seeks to identify representatives of the least advantaged *group*. There are two immediate and related problems with this procedure: first, it requires that groups be identified in some satisfactory way; and second, it requires that, unless everyone in a group is identical, the representative of that group be identified in some satisfactory way. Rawls does not address either of these questions. However, he does note that there may be many possible groups, for example, 'not only are there farmers, say, but dairy farmers, wheat farmers, farmers working on large tracts of land, and so on for other occupations and groups indefinitely', and that 'we cannot have a coherent and manageable theory if we must take such a multiplicity of positions into account'. Rawls also notes that 'the definition of representative men for judging social and economic inequalities is less satisfactory'[33] than for judging other matters. Without any principled way of defining groups, and of identifying representatives within groups, Rawls's procedure must be arbitrary: there would appear to be no reason not to consider individuals rather than representatives of groups. As Van Parijs asks, 'do we not face again an irreducible arbitrariness, which gives no more than a pragmatic justification to stopping short of individuals?'.[34]

Regardless of how groups are defined, only some groups are to be considered. Specifically, Rawls admits only those groups whose members have 'physical needs and psychological capacities within the normal range'.[35] This restriction sits particularly uneasily in a theory of justice that seeks to favour the least advantaged. Surely those whose capacities are below the 'normal range' are precisely those whom such a theory should seek to benefit? As Nozick asks, 'why exclude the group of depressives or alcoholics or the representative paraplegic?'.[36] Equally importantly, it adds yet another arbitrary aspect to the theory. If the 'normal range' excludes the bottom 1 per cent, we have one distribution, if it excludes the bottom 5 per cent, we have a different distribution (not to mention more poor unfortunates who are excluded from consideration).

Primary goods

The wellbeing of representatives is assessed by their allocation of what Rawls terms primary goods. There are two classes of primary goods. The first class comprises social primary goods, such as liberty (the subject matter of the first part of the second principle of justice) and wealth (the subject matter of the second part of that principle), which are available to society to distribute. The second class comprises natural primary goods, such as personal characteristics, which society cannot influence. Justice as fairness is concerned with the distribution of social primary goods; and of these the difference principle is concerned with those that are the subject matter of the second part of the second principle of justice, such as wealth.

Primary goods are 'things which it is supposed a rational man wants whatever else he wants': regardless of what precise things someone might want 'it is assumed that there are various things which he would prefer more of rather than less'.[37] The immediate problem with this characterization is that one 'rational man' may want some things and another may want others. As Sen argues, 'the primary goods approach seems to take little note of the diversity of human beings', for 'people seem to have very different needs'.[38] More specifically, according to Rawls, 'primary social goods, to give them in broad categories, are rights, liberties, and opportunities, and income and wealth'. These fall into two classes: the first comprises rights, liberties, and opportunities; and the second, which is the concern of the difference principle, income and wealth. The essential difference between these classes is that 'liberties and opportunities are defined by the rules of major institutions and the distribution of income and wealth is regulated by them'.[39]

While it is clear that rights and liberties fall into the first class, and income and wealth into the second, the position of opportunities is not as clear. My opportunities are defined by the set of options from which I can choose: for example, working 30 hours a week, having an adequate diet, living in a house, and so forth. But these options are simply facets of my income and wealth (which Rawls clearly construes in real terms not just as sums of money). Thus we may either be concerned with opportunities, or we may be concerned with income and wealth, but to include both in a list of primary goods is to introduce some double counting, and, indeed, confusion.

Further, Rawls does not make clear what is meant by income and wealth, and, indeed, why both are included. In one sense, income is just the yield of wealth, and wealth is just the capitalization of income. It is not clear whether my income comprises the goods and service that I do in fact consume, or those that I could consume if I worked for 30 hours, or 100 hours (the number must be arbitrary) a week, that is, whether it takes account of my leisure time. It is also not clear whether my wealth comprises just my external wealth, such as my house, or whether it also includes my human wealth, such as the skills that I may have acquired.

The index problem

Rawls notes (under the heading of 'several difficulties') that 'one problem clearly is the construction of an index of primary social goods'. This problem is that income and wealth comprise a number of disparate things, such as housing, food, leisure, education and so forth, each available at different times, and that these cannot immediately be aggregated into a composite index. The problem of the construction of an index of primary social goods is not that of combining the primary goods in the first class (rights and liberties) with those in second (income and wealth): because of the lexical ordering of the two principles of justice, and of the two parts of the second principle, the primary goods of the first class may be dealt with independently of those of the second. As Rawls notes 'assuming that the two principles of justice are serially ordered, this problem is greatly simplified'.[40]

Rather, the problem is that of constructing an index of the components of the second class. This is central to the difference principle as the least advantaged member of society is construed as being the member with the lowest index of primary goods. Rawls proposes to construct such an index 'by taking up the standpoint of the representative individual from this group and asking which combination of primary social goods it would be rational for him to prefer'. Rawls accepts that 'in doing this we admittedly rely upon intuitive estimates', but he does not mention the more fundamental problem that this introduces an entirely subjective conception of the good. By 'rational' in this context Rawls does not just mean consistent. He means in accord with some independent conception of what is right: 'it is natural to think that what is right is not a matter of mere preference, and therefore one tries to find a definite conception of the good'.[41] Rawls's index, then, and thus the identity of the least advantaged members of society, depends on this arbitrary conception of the good. Suppose that I have more housing than you but less food. Then if food is deemed to be a higher good than housing, and thus given a higher weight, I may be less advantaged than you; but if housing is deemed to be a higher good than food then you may be less advantaged than me.

Given some conception of the good, Rawls proposes a simplification of the index problem, claiming that 'the only index problem that concerns us is that for the least advantaged group'. This is because 'it is unnecessary to define weights for the more favored positions in any detail, as long as we are sure that they are more favored', and 'this is easy since they frequently have more of each primary good that is distributed unequally'. Accordingly, 'the index problem largely reduces, then, to that of weighting primary goods for the least advantaged'.[42]

This proposed simplification presents a number of problems. One is that it can only apply where those in 'the least advantaged group' have less of every primary good than anyone else. To simplify matters we may consider the case where this group has only one member (if it has more than one member matters are even more difficult). Then it is far from obvious that the least advantaged would have less of every primary good than anyone else. More importantly, whether or not that is the case depends on the arbitrary way in which primary goods are specified. If the primary goods are food and housing I may have less than everyone else, but if they are bread, vegetables, fruit, meat, and so forth I may not; and if they are white bread, brown bread, wholemeal bread, ciabatta, and so forth I almost certainly will not. It is clearly unsatisfactory that the procedure depends on the arbitrary classification of primary goods.

A related problem is that under a fine classification of primary goods the amount of one primary good that Rawls's 'rational man' wants may depend on how much of another good he has. Goods may be substitutes, in that the more white bread I have the less brown bread I want; or they may be complements, in that the more bread I have the more butter I want. But under a coarser classification this may not apply: the amount of food I want may be independent of how much housing I have.

If the least advantaged do not have less of every primary good than everyone else then it will be necessary to define weights for the more favoured positions, and since this possibility is raised it is clear that the weights for these positions may differ from those for the less favoured positions. But this leads to circularity, for *the least favoured member of society can be identified only once the weights for all positions are specified.* Suppose that I have 10 units of housing and 22 of food, and that you have 12 of housing and 18 of food, so that neither of us has less of *each* good than the other. Further suppose that in the least favoured position a weight of ½ is allocated each good, and in the most favoured position a weight of ⅔ is allocated to housing and a weight of ⅓ to food. Then which of us is the least favoured? If I am then I have an index level of 16 (calculated at least favoured position weights as ½ × 10 + ½ × 22) but you have an index level of 14 (calculated at most favoured position weights as ⅔ × 12 + ⅓ × 18), so you are the least favoured. Similarly, if you are the least favoured then you have an index level of 15 but I have an index level of 14, so I am the least favoured. Such a procedure is incoherent.

Robustness

However much Rawls attempts to avoid the problem of interpersonal comparisons of wellbeing, for example, in claiming that 'the difference principle introduces a simplification for the basis of interpersonal comparisons',[43] the fundamental problem remains: the identification of the worst-off essentially involves interpersonal comparisons of wellbeing, and these cannot be made without imposing some arbitrary conception of the good. Rawls attempts to avoid the problems of interpersonal comparisons of utility by employing an index of primary goods rather than a specification of how utilities are assigned. However, the problems remain, for Rawls's index of primary goods is, in effect, a special case of a utility assignment.

Perhaps to circumvent these problems Rawls proposes two ad hoc specifications of the least advantaged. The first of these 'is to choose a particular social position, say that of the unskilled worker, and then to count as the least favored all those with approximately the income and wealth of those in this position, or less'. The obvious problem with this is that there may be a large range of unskilled workers, with widely differing levels of income and, particularly, wealth. The second specification is that 'all persons with less than half of the median may be regarded as the least advantaged segment'. The criterion is 'in terms of relative income and wealth', but, again, income and wealth are illegitimately conflated: in a typical society the distribution of wealth will be far more skewed than the distribution of income. In any event, each of these proposals is arbitrary and lacks any conceptual foundation: why consider all those with less than half the median rather than those with less than a quarter, or those in the bottom 10, or 20, per cent? As Rawls accepts, 'it seems impossible to avoid a certain arbitrariness in actually identifying the least favored group'; any such procedure 'is bound to be somewhat ad hoc'.[44]

A more formal requirement that relates to the identity of the least advantaged is that if a distribution is considered to be just and some members of society leave, taking their primary goods with them, then the distribution among the remaining members of society should be considered to be just. This criterion is that the principle not be what Nozick calls 'organic';[45] it corresponds, in the context of social choice, to Sen's alpha requirement: 'if x is best in a whole set, then it must be best in subsets also'.[46] The difference principle does not satisfy this requirement, for if the least advantaged leave the society then the resulting distribution may not maximize the wellbeing of the new least advantaged: it may be that it was not possible to transfer resources from the most advantaged to the original least advantaged, but it is possible to transfer such resources to the new least advantaged.

A connected requirement, though not as closely related to the identity of the least advantaged, is that if the distribution D1 is considered to be just in one society and D2 is considered to be just in a second (disjoint) society then the distribution that combines D1 and D2 should be just in the new society formed by combining the two original societies. This criterion is what Nozick calls 'the addition condition';[47] it is related, though not identical, to Sen's beta requirement: 'if two alternatives are both best in a subset, then one of them should not be best in the whole set without the other also being best in that set'.[48] The difference principle does not satisfy this requirement either. It may be that everyone in the first society had an index level of 1 and everyone in the second had an index level of 3, but everyone in the new society could have an index level of 2: this would be more just than some in that society having an index level of 1 and the remainder having an index level of 3.

Choice behind the veil

As has been noted, Rawls claims that rational contractors will, from behind a veil of ignorance, adopt his two principles of justice, and in particular the principle that all inequalities 'are to be to the greatest benefit of the least advantaged members of society'. Three matters to consider are the nature of this maximin choice, its special features, and its application to institutions rather than distributions.

Maximin choice

Each contractor considers all feasible distributions of primary goods and chooses one. Because the contractors have been stripped of all distinguishing characteristics they all make the same choice, so we may consider there to be only one contractor. The distributions that this contractor considers allocate different amounts of primary goods to different positions, not to named persons. The contractor's choice is based on 'the assumption of mutually disinterested rationality':

> The persons in the original position try to acknowledge principles which advance their system of ends as far as possible. They do this by attempting to win for themselves the highest index of primary social goods, since this enables them to promote their conception of the good most effectively whatever it turns out to be. The parties do not seek to confer benefits or to impose injuries on one another; they are not moved by affection or rancor. Nor do they try to gain relative to each other; they are not envious.[49]

The contractor does not know which position he will occupy, and as he is aware that he may occupy the least advantaged position he chooses the distribution that allocates the highest index of primary goods to that position. That is, he chooses the distribution that maximizes the index of the least advantaged, or minimum, position. Rawls thus considers his 'two principles as the maximin solution to the problem of social justice' since 'the maximin rule tells us to rank alternatives by their worst possible outcomes: we are to adopt the alternative the worst outcome of which is superior to the worst outcomes of the others'.[50] (However, elsewhere Rawls says that 'economics may wish to refer to the difference principle as the maximin criterion, but I have carefully avoided this name'.[51])

As Rawls observes, 'there is a relation between the two principles and the maximin rule for choice under uncertainty'. But he also accepts that 'the maximin rule is not, in general, a suitable guide for choices under uncertainty'.[52] Rawls insists that the contractor chooses rationally, as in 'the assumption of mutually disinterested rationality'. Indeed, as noted in Chapter 1, he emphasizes that 'the theory of justice is a part, perhaps the most significant part, of the theory of rational choice'; and as he continues, ascertaining the principles that the contractor chooses 'connects the theory of justice with the theory of rational choice'.[53] Accordingly, 'the veil of ignorance leads directly to the problem of choice under complete uncertainty'. (Confusingly, Rawls also states that 'it is possible to regard the parties as perfect altruists and to assume that they reason as if they are certain to be in the position of each person', which interpretation 'removes the element of risk and uncertainty'.[54] Further, this is inconsistent with his requirement that 'the parties do not seek to confer benefits … on one another'.)

Perhaps the greatest single problem with Rawls's theory of justice is that rational contractors will not, except in a most extreme case, choose the maximin outcome. Despite Rawls claiming that 'extreme attitudes to risk are not postulated'[55] it seems unavoidable to conclude that they are, and thus that to choose the maximin distribution is to display the most extreme aversion to risk. It is to refuse to cross the road to buy a newspaper because there is a one in a billion chance of being run over if one does so. In global terms, it is to prefer the distribution of world income in which 7 billion people have just $1 above a widely accepted subsistence income level of $365 a year to the distribution in which all of these except one (who has $365 a year) have the income of the average Luxembourger with $80,000 a year. It is to choose a world of universal abject poverty over one of comfortable affluence for all but one person. This lacks, to put it mildly, intuitive appeal. As Roemer expresses it, 'the choice, by such a [representative] soul, of a Rawlsian tax scheme is hardly justified by rationality, for there seems no good reason to endow the soul with preferences that are, essentially, infinitely risk averse'.[56]

More formally, choosing rationally under uncertainty means choosing in the manner discussed in Chapter 1. Note that the state dependency problem mentioned in that discussion does not arise because of Rawls's assumption that the contractors attempt 'to win for themselves the highest index of primary social goods' irrespective of any other aspects of the distribution, so that they care only about their own positions. Thus the way in which utilities are assigned to index levels is independent of the distribution being considered.

If there are only a few discrete feasible distributions it is logically possible, even if unlikely, that the contractor will choose a maximin distribution. Suppose that there are just two distributions, one that allocates indices of 0 and 9 to the two possible positions, and a second that allocates the index of 4 to each. Suppose further that the utility which I assign to an index level is the square root of that level, and that I assign a probability of ½ to each position. Then I prefer the second, maximin, distribution to the first, even though the first offers more primary goods in total. However, when there is, as Rawls envisages, a continuous range of distributions, the contractor cannot logically choose the maximin distribution. As noted in Chapter 1, one of the axioms of rational choice is a continuity axiom, which requires, in the present context, that it always be possible to offset a small decrease in the index level for one position by an increase in the level for some other position. As Roemer, in the context of social welfare functions, proves more formally, 'continuity eliminates one of the egalitarian contenders … the "leximin" mechanism'.[57] Accordingly, if the contractor chooses rationally, as Rawls insists, and if there is a continuum of possible distributions, then he *cannot* choose the maximin distribution. As Harsanyi expresses it, 'Rawls makes the technical mistake of basing his analysis on a highly irrational decision rule, the maximin principle', which has 'absurd practical implications'.[58]

If instead of presuming that the contractors were infinitely risk averse it were presumed that they were risk neutral then they would choose the distribution which produced the greatest amount of primary goods in total. Under plausible assumptions on incentives, such as those noted above, this would imply that they chose an institution in which there was no redistribution. Thus the assumption of infinite risk aversion implies a significantly egalitarian outcome, while the assumption of risk neutrality implies a more laissez-faire one.

Special features

Rawls appreciates that 'there is a relation between the two principles and the maximin rule for choice under uncertainty', and accepts that 'clearly the maximin rule is not, in general, a suitable guide for choices under uncertainty'. However, he claims that it is a suitable guide if certain features obtain, and seeks to show that 'the original position has these features to a very high degree'.[59] Rawls identifies three such features.

The first is that 'since the rule takes no account of the likelihoods of the possible circumstances, there must be some reason for sharply discounting estimates of these probabilities'.[60] In this Rawls seeks to draw an unwarranted distinction between rational choice under 'risk' and that under 'uncertainty': 'in the case of risk, there is some objective evidential basis for estimating probabilities … in the case of uncertainty there is no such objective basis … we view the parties as faced with uncertainty rather than risk'.[61] As the discussion in Chapter 1 made clear, in the context of choice, all probabilities are simply numerical representations of degrees of belief.

Pettit draws a distinction between Rawls's thick veil of ignorance and a thinner veil. Behind Rawls's veil individuals know that their social and economic positions will depend, at least to some extent, on their personal characteristics, such as their talents, but they do not know what their personal characteristics will be. Behind a thinner veil individuals know that they will be assigned one of a number of social and economic positions but they do not know which. As Pettit argues, the thin veil is sufficient for Rawls's conclusions, and under that veil the contractors (which he calls POPs) may plausibly be presumed to assign the same probability to each position: 'the thin veil would allow the POP's [sic] to reason that they each have the same chance of being in any given social station, the thick would force them to recognize that their chances vary, although in an unknown pattern'.[62] More precisely, if there were n positions the contractor may plausibly be supposed to assign the probability of $1/n$ to each. However, the basis on which the contractors may assign probabilities is immaterial.

The second feature that Rawls identifies is that 'the person choosing has a conception of the good such that he cares very little, if anything, for what he might gain above the minimum stipend that he can, in fact, be sure of by following the maximin rule'.[63] If this is taken to mean that the contractor cares little, but does care something, then nothing changes. (Indeed, the concept of caring little introduces cardinality into the measurement of wellbeing, which Rawls rightly is at pains to avoid.) If this is taken to mean that the contractor does not care at all then it is not clear why we should be concerned with distributive justice. No one (since everyone is the same) would prefer more than the minimum he could be assured of: everyone would be sated with primary goods. In this utopian world there would be no scarcity: distributive justice would be an irrelevance. Further, such a claim is inconsistent with Rawls's definition of primary goods as 'things which it is supposed a rational man wants whatever else he wants', and with his assuming that 'in order to pursue their ends they [the contractors] each prefer a larger to a lesser share'.[64]

The third feature is that 'the rejected alternatives have outcomes that one can hardly accept'.[65] Caring substantially about a decrease in primary goods, just as caring only a little about an increase, changes nothing. In the example of crossing the road to buy a newspaper there are, if I cross the road, two possible outcomes: I may happily acquire a newspaper, or I may die mangled beneath the wheels of a bus. The second of these is not a particularly appealing outcome, and may well be one I 'can hardly accept'. But this does not mean that I will never cross a road.

In summary, none of these three features appears to go any way to justify the choice by a rational contractor of the maximin distribution. Roemer goes further: 'the Rawlsian system is inconsistent and cannot be coherently reconstructed'.[66]

Institutions

The discussion above has been in terms of choosing a distribution. But the contractors do not choose a distribution explicitly; rather, they choose an institution, typically a system of taxes and transfers, which brings about some distribution. The liberties specified in Rawls's first principle ensure that the members of society are not directed as to how much they must work, or what they must consume; rather, they are given an institution and choose their life plans 'to win for themselves the highest index of primary social goods' in the light of this. Now just as any chosen distribution must be feasible so must any institution: for a system of taxes and transfers this requires that the total distributed be the same as the total collected. (Clearly the sum distributed cannot exceed what is collected; it could be less than this, but that would not be consistent with a maximin outcome, for the excess could be distributed to the least advantaged.) There is here a fundamental difficulty: I cannot choose an institution unless I know how you will respond to it, for your and others' responses will determine whether or not the institution is feasible. If a high tax rate deters you from working there will be less to distribute to others than if it does not. But I do not know how you will respond. The veil of ignorance requires that 'the parties do not know the particular circumstances of their own society', and that 'they do not know its economic or political situation'. This would appear to be a fundamental problem with Rawls's social contract approach.

An example showing how contractors may choose an institution, rather than choose a distribution explicitly, is given in the appendix to this chapter. This example also illustrates the difference between the institution that the contractors choose and the maximin institution.

Alternative arguments

Although the contract argument is Rawls's main argument for the difference principle Rawls also suggests two alternative arguments, one based on mutual advantage and one based on stability and related properties.

Mutual advantage

The first argument may be seen as a parallel to Barry's view that 'justice is simply rational prudence pursued in contexts where the cooperation (or at least forbearance) of other people is a condition of our being able to get what we want'. Barry terms this interpretation 'justice as mutual advantage'; this is contrasted with 'justice as impartiality', which is the view that 'a just state of affairs is one that people can accept not merely in the sense that they cannot reasonably *expect* to get more, but in the stronger sense that they cannot reasonably *claim* more'.[67] Justice as impartiality is the justice of Rawls's contract theory; while this requires a theory of fairness, justice as mutual advantage, in contrast, requires a theory of bargaining.

Rawls approaches justice as mutual advantage by considering someone in the original position, and suggests that 'since it is not reasonable for him to expect more than an equal share in the division of social primary goods, and since it is not rational for him to agree to less', he will 'acknowledge as the first step a principle of justice requiring an equal distribution'. Rawls claims that 'this principle is so obvious given the symmetry of the parties that it would occur to everyone immediately'. However, that is not the end of the story, for the members of society would appreciate that there were alternative arrangements that would benefit everyone: 'if there are inequalities in income and wealth … that work to make everyone better off in comparison with the benchmark of equality, why not permit them?'. No one would have any reason for objecting to such an alternative arrangement. The only reason they might have for objecting is envy, but Rawls explicitly rules this out: the parties 'decide as if they are not moved by envy'. Then 'because the parties start from an equal division of all social primary goods, those who benefit least have, so to speak, a veto'. Accordingly, Rawls claims, 'we arrive at the difference principle'.[68]

This final claim seems unjustified. If the parties start from a position of equality it is indeed plausible that they will make changes to their situations that they each consider to be advantageous, that is, adopt a Pareto superior alternative. But this does not imply that they will adopt a maximin alternative. Even if the maximin distribution is a Pareto efficient distribution there will typically be many other Pareto efficient distributions. Suppose that in an equal distribution, $D1$, you and I each have 1 unit of some good. By cooperation we could achieve the distribution $D2$ in which you have 4 units and I have 2; or we could achieve the distribution $D3$ in which you have 3 units and I have 4 (but can achieve no other distribution). Then each of $D2$ and $D3$ is Pareto superior to $D1$, and indeed a Pareto efficient distribution, but $D2$ is not a maximin distribution. More seriously, as is shown above, the maximin distribution may not even be a Pareto efficient (in the standard sense) distribution. Thus an argument that the parties will make changes to their situations that they each consider to be advantageous is not an argument that they will adopt a maximin distribution. Those who benefit least do indeed have a veto, but this does not aid the argument: since the changes are required to be mutually advantageous everyone has a veto.

(It might be noted in passing that Rawls's ruling out any expression of envy seems unwarranted; and no justification is given for this assumption. Envy and greed, at least in the view of Klein,[69] are the two fundamental poles of the psyche, even if they are usually expressed in socially acceptable forms. Rawls recognizes the socially acceptable form of greed: as noted, he assumes that the members of society 'each prefer a larger to a lesser share'. There is an unexplained asymmetry in accepting one of these poles but not the other.)

A possible way of supporting Rawls's claim is through what Martin calls 'the Pareto efficient-egalitarian version of the difference principle', which 'could serve as a bridge between the simple idea of "everybody's advantage" or of mutual benefit and the stronger notion of "the greatest benefit of the least advantaged"'.[70] This first requires that the Pareto principle be satisfied, and then introduces an egalitarian constraint which, in effect, specifies that the inequality between the most advantaged and the least advantaged is to be minimized. As Martin shows, if there are only two classes then this version of the difference principle is equivalent to Rawls's version. However, if there are more than two classes this will only be the case if Rawls's chain-connection assumption is satisfied.

A potential confusion in the mutual advantage argument arises because there are two conceptions of mutual advantage. By cooperating, the members of society may obtain a larger bundle of primary goods than they have when these goods are equally distributed: justice may involve allocating *the new bundle* in some fair way, or it may involve allocating the gains from cooperation, that is *the increase in the bundle*, in some fair way. What is seen as being just under the first interpretation may not be seen as being just under the second, and vice versa. Rawls's contractual argument interprets justice in the first way, that is, in terms of the new bundle itself, but in the mutual advantage argument it would be more natural to interpret justice in the second way, that is, in terms of the gains from cooperation. If there were one fixed index of primary goods the two interpretations would be the same: if everyone starts with the same index level and I have gained the least then my new index level is the least, and vice versa. However, this may not be the case if, as it does in Rawls's framework, my index depends on my position.

Stability

Rawls's second alternative argument is that there are three requirements, and particularly that of stability, which any principles of justice must meet, and that his principles meet these requirements, or at least meet them more closely than do any other conceptions of justice.

The first of these requirements is that the parties to the contract 'can rely on one another to adhere to the principles adopted'. As the social contract is final the parties to it will have no second chance. They must, then, 'weigh with care whether they will be able to stick by their commitment in all circumstances'. Rawls claims that his principles meet this requirement because 'not only do the parties protect their basic rights but they insure themselves against the worst eventualities'.[71]

The second requirement of a conception of justice is that 'it generates its own support', that is, in Rawls's terminology, that it is stable. What is meant by this is that when people live under certain principles of justice for any length of time they develop a desire to act in accordance with those principles: 'a conception of justice is stable when the public recognition of its realization by the social system tends to bring about the corresponding sense of justice'. Stability is ensured, it is claimed, through the workings of 'the psychological law that persons tend to love, cherish, and support whatever affirms their own good', and 'since everyone's good is affirmed, all acquire inclinations to uphold the scheme'.[72]

The third requirement of a conception of justice is that 'it should publicly express men's respect for one another'. Rawls claims that his principles meet this requirement because 'when society follows these principles, everyone's good is included in a scheme of mutual benefit and this public affirmation in institutions of each man's endeavors supports men's self-esteem'.[73]

It is not clear that Rawls's principles do in fact meet these requirements, or at least the first and the third of these, or even meet them more closely than any other conception of justice. This is partly because it is not clear precisely what these requirements mean, and partly because the main conception with which Rawls contrasts his principles is utilitarianism, a theory that Rawls roundly dismisses elsewhere.

It is the second of these requirements that Rawls considers to be the most important, and develops further in *Political Liberalism* and elsewhere. A conception of justice is now considered to be stable if 'those who grow up in a society well-ordered by it ... develop a sufficient allegiance to those [its] institutions ... so that they normally act as justice requires, provided they are assured that others will act likewise'.[74] Thus a conception is stable if it is stable in the sense that a Nash equilibrium is stable: no individual has an incentive to deviate from it. But it is important that the reason why no members of society would deviate is not that they might not gain, but that they have internalized its precepts:

> As a liberal conception, justice as fairness must not merely avoid futility; the explanation of why it is practicable must be of a special kind. The problem of stability is not the problem of bringing others who reject a conception to share it, or to act in accordance with it by workable sanctions if necessary – as if the task were to find ways to impose that conception on others once we are ourselves convinced it is sound. Rather, as a liberal political conception, justice as fairness relies for its reasonableness in the first place upon generating its own support in a suitable way by addressing each citizen's reason, as explained within its own framework.[75]

The two principles of justice are stable because they generate an overlapping consensus, that is, 'a consensus in which a diversity of conflicting comprehensive doctrines endorse the same political conception, in this case, justice as fairness'.[76] However, it remains unclear why this is the case. A partial answer is that the members of society are presumed to have 'the two moral powers, one a capacity for a sense of justice and the other a capacity for a conception of the good'.[77] However, no basis for this presumption is given.

Emphasizing stability, however, creates its own problems. Rawls's discussion employs the concept of feasible distributions without distinguishing, as Cohen[78] implicitly, and Roemer[79] explicitly, do, between two interpretations of this concept. Under the first interpretation the set of feasible distributions comprises all those that are technologically possible: these are all the distributions that an omnipotent state could impose. Under the second interpretation the set of feasible distributions is the subset of this first set comprising the distributions that a liberal state could properly impose. This second set is smaller than the first because the proper power of the state is restricted by the first of the two principles of justice, and in particular by the ability of individuals to make their own decisions, on such matters such as how much to work, in the light of whatever redistribution scheme the state imposes.

Suppose that $D1$ is the distribution that maximizes the wellbeing of the least advantaged over the first set of feasible distributions, and that $D2$ is the distribution that maximizes the wellbeing of the least advantaged over the second set. Rawls interprets $D2$ as being the just distribution, but Cohen argues that Rawls can only consistently interpret $D1$ as the just distribution.

Achieving the distribution $D2$ will, in general, involve giving the more talented incentives to work more. This in turn will imply that those with more talents, the distribution of which, in Rawls's framework, is considered to be morally arbitrary, will receive more primary goods than those with fewer talents. (In this context having more talents means nothing more than fortuitously having a capacity for high earnings: the more talented are simply those who '*are so positioned that, happily, for them, they do command a high salary and they can vary their productivity according to exactly how high it is*'.[80]) Rawls claims that the resulting inequality in $D2$ is justified because of the difference principle. Cohen maintains that considering $D2$ to be just contradicts the basis of Rawls's position, that the distribution of talents is morally arbitrary and thus should not affect the basic principle that equality requires an equal distribution of primary goods. (It might be noted in passing that both Rawls's and Cohen's assumption that the distribution of talents is morally arbitrary becomes less appealing if some talents are developed by their possessors.)

In the distribution $D2$ the talented are not embracing the conditions of justice that they are supposed to embrace, namely, that society should be organized so as to benefit the least advantaged: they are consenting to enjoy more primary goods than others simply on account of morally arbitrary factors. Either the talented affirm the difference principle or they do not. If they do not, then $D2$ is not just because justice requires that the members of society affirm the principles of justice. This is the stability requirement. If the talented do affirm the difference principle then 'as Rawls says, they apply the principles of justice *in their daily life* and achieve a sense of their own justice in doing so'.[81] They may reasonably accept the inequalities from which they benefit if these are necessary to benefit the least advantaged, but 'necessary' has two meanings in this context, which meanings correspond to the two meanings of feasible discussed above. It may mean as dictated by the technology, as in the first sense of feasible; or it may mean as constrained by individual choices (made in the light of whatever redistribution scheme is in place) as to how much to work and so forth, as in the second sense of feasible. Rawls's position requires the second interpretation; Cohen argues for the first. As Cohen concludes,

> This double-minded modeling of the implementation of the difference principle, with citizens inspired by justice endorsing a state policy which plays a tax game against (some of) them in their manifestation as self-seeking economic agents, is wholly out of accord with the (sound) Rawlsian requirement on a just society that its citizens themselves willingly submit to the standard of justice embodied in the difference principle.[82]

Conclusions

The strength of Rawls's theory of justice as fairness lies in its combination of the fundamental notion of equality with the requirement of Pareto efficiency.

However, the theory has a number of problems. Some of these may be avoided by inessential changes. For example, the incoherence of the variable index of primary goods may be avoided by using a single index; and the impossibility of choosing a feasible distribution when the contractors do not know others' responses may be avoided by adopting a thin rather than a thick veil of ignorance. But other problems are unavoidable, particularly that of identifying the least advantaged (with the related problems of defining primary goods and the construction of an index of these), and that of the supposedly rational choice of the maximin principle with its 'absurd practical implications'.

Rawls's theory cannot properly be criticized for only recognizing a restricted form of liberty for it is explicitly an egalitarian theory. But it is worth noting the extent of this restriction. To give but one example, it requires 'society [to act as] as employer of last resort through general or local government'.[83] This implies that if I am not otherwise employed you would be compelled, through the agency of the government, to employ, and pay, me to do something that you did not consider to be worthwhile: if you had considered it worthwhile then you would have employed me without the need for compulsion. This is hardly a Pareto improvement. (Rawls is not considering public goods, that is goods that people want collectively but no one is prepared to pay for individually: he makes it clear that such goods are to be provided anyway, not just as a 'last resort'.)

Rawls seeks to 'preserve an approximate justice in distributive shares by means of taxation and the necessary adjustments in the rights of property'.[84] As regards taxation he proposes expenditure or income taxes (preferring the former, despite the fact that the two are equivalent, apart from timing). Income taxes are clearly inconsistent with self-ownership, which involves full rights to the fruits of one's labour, and a tax on income is a violation of that right (even if it is not, as Nozick claims, 'on a par with forced labor'[85]). And making adjustments to the rights of property is clearly inconsistent with resource-ownership, which involves full rights to own external resources and the produce of these. Further, personal responsibility is not recognized in that adjustments are made for inequalities that are the result of individuals' choices, and specifically those between consumption and leisure, for which they are deemed to be responsible.

In summary, as indicated in Chapter 1, justice as fairness maintains neither full self-ownership nor full resource-ownership, and does not recognize individual responsibility.

Appendix

This example, a discrete version of a continuous example given by Roemer,[86] illustrates how the contractors may choose an institution, as a system of taxes and transfers, rather than choose a distribution explicitly. It also illustrates the difference between the institution that the contractors choose and the maximin institution.

There are two primary goods, consumption and leisure. The index of primary goods is given by a utility function, the arguments of which are consumption and labour (labour being the obverse of leisure). Institutions are taxes on income: the tax that a member of society bears may be positive or negative. A tax is feasible if its net proceeds are zero.

More specifically, there are n workers, labelled by $w = 0 \ldots n - 1$. The worker labelled w has a real wage of w, so that if his labour is x then his pre-tax income y is wx. The tax schedule t is linear, and is given by $t(y) = \alpha + \beta y$, where $0 \leq \beta \leq 1$. Then if a worker's labour is x his post-tax income, and thus his consumption, c, is $(1 - \beta)wx - \alpha$. All workers have the same preferences between consumption and labour, represented by their assigning the utility level of $c - \frac{1}{2}x^2$ to the combination comprising the consumption c and the labour x. Utility is increasing in consumption and decreasing in labour (and thus increasing in leisure).

Given the tax schedule t, the worker w will choose his labour x so as to maximize $(1 - \beta)wx - \alpha - \frac{1}{2}x^2$. This implies that $x = (1 - \beta)w$: his consumption is $w^2\beta(1 - \beta)^2 - \alpha$, his utility level is $\frac{1}{2}w^2\beta(1 - \beta)^2 - \alpha$, and his tax is $\alpha + w^2\beta(1 - \beta)$.

The feasibility condition, that the net proceeds of the tax be zero, is the condition that $\sum[\alpha + w^2\beta(1 - \beta)] = 0$, where this (and all) summation is over $w = 0$ to $n - 1$. This implies that $\alpha = -\beta(1 - \beta)\sum w^2/n$, so that the tax system may be represented by β alone.

The tax system that maximizes the wellbeing of the least advantaged is that given by

$$\max_\beta \min_w [\tfrac{1}{2}w^2\beta(1 - \beta)^2 + \beta(1 - \beta)\sum w^2/n].$$

The solution of this problem is $\beta = \frac{1}{2}$: the maximin institution would have a marginal tax rate of 50 per cent.

However, if a typical worker w chooses the level of β that maximizes his expected utility he chooses the level that maximizes

$$E[\tfrac{1}{2}(1 - \beta)^2w^2 - \alpha] = \tfrac{1}{2}(1 - \beta)^2 Ew^2 + \beta(1-\beta)Ew^2.$$

The solution of this problem is $\beta = 0$, which implies that $\alpha = 0$, so that there is no redistribution whatsoever.

Thus the members of society choose an institution that differs radically from the maximin institution. No risk aversion is built into this example, but a more complicated argument leads to a similar result for any (finite) level of risk aversion.

Notes

1 All references in this chapter that do not specify an author are to Rawls (1999a).
2 Page 24.
3 Rawls (2005), pages 5–6.
4 Rawls (2005), pages 6–7.
5 Page xviii.
6 Page 11.
7 Nozick (1974), page 287.
8 Dworkin (1977), page 151.
9 Page 19.
10 Dworkin (1981), page 345.

11 Harsanyi (1953).
12 Sidgwick (1874/1981), 3.2.3, page 209.
13 Page 118.
14 Smith (1759/2002), 3.3.7, page 160.
15 Page 161.
16 Kymlicka (2002), page 63.
17 Pages 16–17.
18 Page 120.
19 Page 121.
20 Page 111.
21 Page 68.
22 Page 68.
23 Rawls (1975), page 257 as reprinted.
24 Rawls (2001), page 71, emphasis added.
25 Page 69.
26 Page 60.
27 Page 58, emphasis added.
28 Page 69, emphasis added.
29 Pages 70–72.
30 Sen (1970a), page 138n.
31 Page 72.
32 Page 72.
33 Pages 82–83.
34 Van Parijs (2003), page 214.
35 Page 83.
36 Nozick (1974), page 190.
37 Page 79.
38 Sen (1980), page 215.
39 Page 79.
40 Page 80.
41 Page 490.
42 Page 80.
43 Page 79.
44 Page 86.
45 Nozick (1974), page 209.
46 Sen (1970a), page 50.
47 Nozick (1974), page 209.
48 Sen (1970a), page 50.
49 Page 125.
50 Pages 132–33.
51 Page 72.
52 Pages 132–33.
53 Page 16.
54 Page 149.
55 Page 73.
56 Roemer (1996), page 181.
57 Roemer (1996), page 136.
58 Harsanyi (1977), page 47 as reprinted.
59 Pages 132–33.
60 Page 134.
61 Rawls (2001), page 106.
62 Pettit (1980), page 173.
63 Page 134.
64 Page 109.

65 Page 134.
66 Roemer (1996), page 182.
67 Barry (1989), pages 6–8.
68 Pages 130–31.
69 Klein (1957), chapter 1.
70 Martin (2012), pages 406–7.
71 Pages 153–54.
72 Pages 154–55.
73 Page 156.
74 Rawls (1989), page 479 as reprinted.
75 Rawls (1989), page 488 as reprinted.
76 Rawls (1989), page 486 as reprinted.
77 Rawls (1989), page 494 as reprinted.
78 Cohen (1997), section 2.
79 Roemer (1996), section 5.4.
80 Cohen (1997), pages 6–7.
81 Cohen (1997), page 8.
82 Cohen (1997), pages 9–10.
83 Rawls (2005), page lviii.
84 Page 245.
85 Nozick (1974), page 169.
86 Roemer (1996), section 5.3.

3

EQUALITY OF RESOURCES

In the framework in which justice is interpreted as laissez-faire with compensation for morally arbitrary factors, equality of resources, as developed by Dworkin,[1] treats individuals' abilities and external resources as arbitrary, but makes no adjustments for their preferences. The essence of this approach is the distinction between ambition-sensitivity, which recognizes differences which are due to differing ambitions, and endowment-sensitivity, which recognizes differences that are due to differing endowments.

Equal resources

Dworkin accepts that inequalities are acceptable if they result from voluntary choices, but not if they result from disadvantages that have not been chosen. However, initial equality of resources is not sufficient for justice. Even if we start from the same position you may fare better than I do because of your good luck, or, alternatively, because of your lesser handicaps or greater talents. The development of a theory of justice based on equal resources requires, then, a discussion of initial resources, of fortune, of handicaps, and of talents.

Initial resources

Dworkin motivates his theory of justice with the example of a number of survivors of a shipwreck who are washed up, with no belongings, on an uninhabited island with abundant natural resources. The survivors accept that these resources should be allocated among them in some equitable fashion, and agree that for a division to be equitable it must meet 'the envy test', which requires that no one 'would prefer someone else's bundle of resources to his own bundle'.[2] It is assumed that each survivor is concerned only with his own bundle, and prefers a larger bundle to a smaller.

The envy test, however, is too weak a test: Dworkin[3] gives two examples of allocations that meet this test but appear inequitable. The underlying problem with the test (which Dworkin does not mention) is that allocations that meet the test may fail to be Pareto efficient. Suppose that there are two resources, wheat and oats, and that you and I have the same preferences: we each are indifferent between a bundle with no wheat and one with no oats, but prefer any bundle with positive amounts of each to either of these extremes. Then the allocation that gives you all the wheat and me all the oats meets the envy test, but we each prefer any allocation that divides the wheat and oats between us.

To avoid the problems he identifies Dworkin proposes that the survivors appoint an auctioneer who gives each of them an equal number of tokens. The auctioneer divides the resources into a number of lots and proposes a system of prices, one for each lot, denominated in tokens. The survivors bid for the lots, with the requirement that their total proposed expenditure in tokens does not exceed their endowment of tokens. If all markets clear, that is, if there is precisely one would-be purchaser for each lot, then the process ends. If all markets do not clear then the auctioneer adjusts the prices (though Dworkin does not specify how), and continues to adjust them until (it is supposed) they do.

The immediate problem with this procedure is that there may be no prices at which the markets clear. If you and I are the only survivors and we have the same preferences then whatever the price of a lot either we will both bid for it or neither of us will: either way, the market will not clear. Because of the discrete nature of the lots this problem may also arise if we have similar preferences. This problem may be avoided if it is supposed that all resources are continuously divisible, as, for example, is water. Prices are now expressed in tokens per unit of the resource, for example, tokens per litre of water, and survivors bid for quantities of each resource. The market for a resource will now clear if the total of the quantities bid for it is equal to the quantity of the resource that is available. If the prices are such that all markets clear the resulting array of bundles that the survivors purchase at these prices is known as a Walrasian equilibrium. As Debreu[4] has shown, there will, at least under some very weak assumptions on the preferences of the survivors, always be some such equilibrium. Since everyone has the same number of tokens this outcome is, more precisely, an equal-wealth Walrasian equilibrium, that is, a Walrasian equilibrium that is reached from an initial state in which everyone has the same wealth. If resources are defined appropriately the assumption that all resources are continuously divisible is not particularly restrictive. For example, instead of defining a rock, with room for only one person, from which fish may be caught to be a resource we may define the use of the rock for a day to be the resource. The rock may not be divisible, but the use of it is.

There may, however, be more than one system of prices at which all markets clear, and indeed infinitely many, but this is immaterial. What is material is that the resulting distribution is Pareto efficient and meets the envy test. To see that it is Pareto efficient suppose that there is some alternative distribution that everyone prefers. But if I prefer my bundle of resources in this alternative distribution why did I not purchase it? The answer must be because I could not afford it, that is, because its value at the given prices was greater than that of my actual bundle. But as all prices are positive this implies that the alternative bundle contains more of at least one resource than my actual bundle does. Since this applies to everyone it follows that the alternative distribution requires more of at least one resource than the original distribution does. And as the original distribution used all the resources available this implies that the alternative distribution is not feasible. (This argument demonstrates that the distribution is Pareto efficient in the weak sense; a slightly lengthier argument on the same lines demonstrates that it is Pareto efficient in the standard sense. This result is known as the First Fundamental Theorem of Welfare Economics: a formal proof is provided by Debreu.[5]) To see that the resulting distribution meets the envy test note that if I preferred your bundle to mine then I would have purchased it: I could have done so because we each have the same number of tokens and we each face the same prices. However, I did not.

To complete the description of the auction process it is necessary to specify a rule for the adjustment of prices if all markets do not clear. A natural rule is that which changes prices in proportion to excess demands, that is, increases the price of a resource if more is bid for than is available and decreases the price if less is bid for than is available, and does each in proportion to the difference. The problem now is that although there will be some prices at which all markets clear, the auction process may not discover these. Suppose that two (of many) resources, X and Y, are complementary, in that X is of little use without Y, and vice versa: then an increase in the price of X would deter purchases of X and accordingly deter purchases of Y. Suppose further that at some prices there is a large excess demand for X and a small excess supply of Y. Then there will be a large increase in the price of X and a small decrease in the price of Y. Together, these may well lead to a fall in the demand for Y, and thus an *increase* in its excess supply. The price adjustment is thus destabilizing. This problem would be critical if, as Dworkin holds, 'the auction is not simply a convenient or ad hoc device' but 'an institutionalized form of the process of discovery and adaptation that is at the center of the ethics of that ideal'.[6] However, this seems unnecessary: it is the outcome, of an equal-wealth Walrasian equilibrium, rather than the process that is central to this conception of justice: as Heath comments, 'the auction is simply a stand-in for a perfectly competitive market, and ... does not appear to be accomplishing much on the equality front'.[7]

There is a good reason why an equal-wealth Walrasian equilibrium may be considered to be equitable in its own right, as will be seen. First, though, note that not all voluntary moves from a position of equal wealth (which is, of course, envy-free) will preserve the envy-free property. Suppose that you, I, and Ronald Dworkin (RD) have the same wealth, and that you and I have the same preferences but RD has different preferences. Then you and RD will be able to make exchanges that benefit each of you, and when you do I will necessarily envy you. The problem with this example is that the symmetry of the initial position is destroyed by the exchanges. The advantage of the Walrasian equilibrium is that it maintains this symmetry, for everyone faces the same prices and therefore has the same opportunities to trade. In fact, in a large society where individuals' tastes vary continuously across the population the *only* outcomes that are both Pareto efficient and meet the envy test are Walrasian equilibria with equal wealth.

To see this, first note that if an outcome is Pareto efficient then it will be a Walrasian equilibrium for some distribution of wealth. Choose some Pareto efficient outcome and let each person's wealth be just sufficient to enable him to purchase the bundle of resources that he holds in this outcome. Then because the outcome is Pareto efficient no one will want to trade, which is to say that the outcome is a Walrasian equilibrium. (This is an instance of the Second Fundamental Theorem of Welfare Economics, a proof of which is provided by Debreu.[8]) Now if everyone has the same preferences then in an envy-free Walrasian equilibrium everyone must have the same wealth: since you and I have the same preferences, and face the same prices, I would envy you if your wealth exceeded mine. This would also apply if my preferences differed only *very* slightly from yours; and under the assumption that preferences vary continuously there will be someone whose preferences do differ very slightly from yours. Thus in all envy-free Walrasian equilibria everyone must have the same wealth. Since every Pareto efficient outcome is a Walrasian equilibrium for some distribution of wealth it follows that all Pareto efficient outcomes that are envy-free are Walrasian equilibria with equal wealth. (A formal proof of this proposition, which requires the topological specification of what 'very slightly' means, is provided by Varian.[9])

Some resources, such as hill land, may require more labour to make them more productive than others, such as meadow land. A problem with Dworkin's envy test is that it considers only physical resources and ignores the labour that is required to make them bear fruit. In this setting there may be no Pareto efficient allocations that meet the envy test. Assume that you are twice as productive as I am, so that the total that we can consume is determined by the hours that I work plus twice the hours that you work, and that you value leisure (relative to consumption) more highly than I. Then Pareto efficiency will require that you do all the work and that I compensate you by allowing you more consumption. But then I will envy you because you consume more than me, and you will envy me because I have more leisure than you. The underlying problem here is that au fond I envy your greater productivity, and there is no way in which this can be removed, any more than my envying your better looks could be removed. (A formal analysis of this example is given by Pazner and Schmeidler.[10]) This problem is critical for Dworkin's approach, but would be immaterial if an equal-wealth Walrasian equilibrium were considered to be equitable in its own right, and, as noted above, there are strong grounds for considering this to be the case.

Fortune

Dworkin seeks to make people responsible for the effects of their choices, but not for matters beyond their control. If you and the footballer George Best (who is alleged to have said 'I spent 90 per cent of my money on women, drink, and fast cars; the rest I wasted') start with the same wealth but you save some of yours while he dissipates his then he has no claim on your greater wealth. However, it may be a different matter if his farm is struck by an unexpected tsunami but yours is not.

To take account of the latter case, Dworkin distinguishes between 'option luck' and 'brute luck'. Option luck is 'a matter of how deliberate and calculated gambles turn out – whether someone gains or loses through accepting an isolated risk he or she should have anticipated and might have declined'. Brute luck is 'a matter of how risks fall out that are not in that sense deliberate gambles'. However, Dworkin accepts that the difference between these two forms of luck is 'a matter of degree'. He gives as an example someone who develops cancer. If this occurs 'in the course of a normal life' this is brute bad luck; but if he has smoked heavily 'then we may prefer to say that he took an unsuccessful gamble'.[11] Insofar as the two can be distinguished, people should be responsible for the outcomes of option luck, but not of brute luck.

There are other problems besides vagueness ('a matter of degree') with Dworkin's distinction between option and brute luck. First, it is not clear what a 'deliberate' gamble is. The effect of any action I take today will depend on the state of the world that emerges tomorrow. In an uncertain world (which is the only world of relevance) I do not know what state this will be. Thus any action (or inaction) necessarily involves risk. If I venture outside without an umbrella and it rains then I get wet; if I take an umbrella and it does not rain then I am unnecessarily hampered. If we are to treat people as rational beings then we must presume that they act deliberately, so that all gambles are deliberate. Second, it is not clear what an 'isolated risk' is, nor why isolation might be relevant. Third, it is not clear what 'should have anticipated' means. It may mean 'should have given some thought to', or it may mean 'having given some thought to assigns an incorrect probability to'. The first interpretation would apply if Dworkin's cancer victim closed his mind to the possibility of contracting cancer; the second would apply if he assigned an 'incorrect' probability to that outcome. The first interpretation would require that, for the reasons mentioned above, he was not a rational being. The second would require that there were some objective, 'correct', probability of his developing cancer. As noted in Chapter 1, there can be no such probability. Finally, continuing with Dworkin's cancer example, the distinction between 'a normal life' and smoking is purely subjective, and arbitrary: no life style removes the risk of all ailments (and death eventually strikes even the most normal).

Dworkin's key argument concerning luck is that 'insurance, so far as it is available, provides a link between brute and option luck, because the decision to buy or reject catastrophe insurance is a calculated gamble'. Then because people should be responsible for the outcomes of option luck they should be responsible for the outcomes of all luck, at least if they could have bought insurance. Dworkin considers the case in which some of the survivors plant valuable but risky crops while others plant safer crops. Some of the former buy insurance against unfavourable weather but others do not. At harvest time, some will have fared better than others. Dworkin asks whether the resulting differences are justified, and (after making not strictly necessary distinctions between those who play it safe, those who gamble and win, and those who gamble and lose) concludes that the principle that 'equality of resources requires that people pay the true cost of the lives that they lead, warrants rather than condemns these differences'. In the light of that Dworkin adds the following rider to his envy test:

> In computing the extent of someone's resources over his life, for the purpose of asking whether anyone else envies those resources, any resources gained through a successful gamble should be represented by the opportunity to take the gamble at the odds in force, and comparable adjustments made to the resources of those who have lost through gambles.[12]

Just as Dworkin's auction process may be represented more simply in terms of an equal-wealth Walrasian equilibrium, his analysis of risks may be represented more simply in terms of an equal-wealth Walrasian equilibrium with contingent commodities. A contingent commodity is one that is available only in a certain state of the world, for example, wheat if the weather has been favourable (in some precisely defined sense, involving temperature and rainfall each day). If I purchase a kilogram of this commodity today and the weather has been favourable then I receive a kilogram of wheat at harvest time; if the weather has not been favourable then I receive nothing. I can purchase a kilogram of wheat tout court by purchasing a kilogram of 'wheat if the weather has been favourable' and a kilogram of 'wheat if the weather has not been favourable'. The use of contingent commodities removes all risks: any 'insurance' is acquired implicitly through the purchase of the appropriate contingent commodities rather than explicitly. Contingent commodities also remove any possible ambiguity in Dworkin's phrase 'insurance, so far as it is available', for all contingent commodities are necessarily available in that it is always possible for people to agree to trade in such commodities, irrespective of whether anyone actually does so. As Debreu[13] shows, there will always be an equal-wealth Walrasian equilibrium with contingent commodities. And again, this is appealing in its own right.

Handicaps

Neither insurance nor contingent commodities can remove all risks. If someone is born blind he cannot buy insurance against blindness. Dworkin seeks to take account of this through a hypothetical insurance scheme. He asks how much an average person would be prepared to pay for insurance against being handicapped if in the initial state everyone had the same, and known, chance of being handicapped. He then supposes that 'the average person would have purchased insurance at that level',[14] and proposes to compensate those who do develop handicaps out of a fund that is collected by taxation but designed to match the fund that would have been provided through insurance premiums. The compensation that someone with a handicap is to receive is the contingent compensation that he would have purchased, knowing the risk of being handicapped, had actual insurance been available. Dworkin's hypothetical insurance scheme in some initial state has some similarity with Rawls's hypothetical contract in the original position. However, Dworkin's veil of ignorance (although he does not use this phrase) is a thin one, behind which individuals are presumed to know their preferences, including their preferences for risk, but not the handicaps that they will have in the initial state. Under this scheme those who develop handicaps will then have more resources than those who do not, but the difference is accounted for by market decisions that everyone is supposed to have made in a position of equality.

There are a number of problems with this procedure. An immediate one is that as probability is subjective it is not clear what everyone having the same, and known, chance of being handicapped means. A further one is that it does not treat everyone equally. Behind the veil everyone knows his preference for risk. Someone with the average aversion to risk will obtain the level of insurance that he would have chosen, but if you are more than averagely risk averse then you will be forced to have less insurance than you would have chosen, and if I am less than averagely risk averse then I will be forced to have more than I would have chosen. Those with a higher or lower risk aversion than the average are forced to enter into contracts that they would not have chosen solely because they have eccentric preferences, even though the scheme is meant to ignore preferences.

However, this aspect of Dworkin's scheme does ensure that a problem which Anderson raises does not apply. Anderson claims that Dworkin's proposal would treat two people with the same disability differently, depending on their tastes: 'a risk-averse blind person could be entitled to aid denied to a risk-loving blind person, on the grounds that the latter probably would not have insured against being blind'. This problem would not arise because it is only what 'the average' person would choose that is relevant. Anderson also claims that 'people who have an extremely rare but severe disability could be ineligible for special aid just because the chances of anyone suffering from it were so minute that it was *ex ante* rational for people not to purchase insurance against it', and accordingly that Dworkin's 'proposal discriminates between people with rare and common disabilities'.[15] However, this too seems misplaced: if the chances were 'so minute' then the premium would be correspondingly minute: there is no more reason why people would insure against unlikely events at a low premium than against likely ones at a high premium (or vice versa).

A further potential problem is that preferences, or ambitions, and handicaps are interrelated. Someone who is born blind will not seek the same lifestyle as a sighted person: the latter may consider being an artist, but not the former. My decision as to how much of my resource to devote to insurance against some handicap will depend on the lifestyles I would seek with and without that handicap. Dworkin observes that 'in order to decide how much insurance such a person would have bought without the handicap we must decide what sort of life he would have planned in that case', and notes that 'there may be no answer, even in principle, to that question'.[16] However, Dworkin may be being unduly pessimistic. If someone is presumed to be able to evaluate the lifestyle of an artist as against that of a musician tout court he may equally be presumed to be able to evaluate the lifestyle of a sighted artist as against that of a blind musician, and to know how much of his resources in the initial situation he would devote to insurance to compensate him for the difference.

Dworkin's separation of handicaps from preferences and ambitions raises a further problem. There are many factors other than handicap that affect my wellbeing but are beyond my control. For example, I may have a taste for some resource that is particularly scarce. As Dworkin asks, 'would it not now be fair to treat as handicaps eccentric tastes, or tastes that are expensive or impossible to satisfy because of scarcity of some good that might have been common?'.[17] Dworkin argues that it would not, for someone with a handicap 'faces his life with what we concede to be fewer resources, just on that account, than others do', which is not the case for someone with expensive tastes. Although it is intuitively clear that blindness is a handicap and a preference for (to use Arrow's well-known example) 'clarets and plovers' eggs'[18] is an expensive taste the position is less clear in other cases. A preference for staying at home rather than going out to work may be just that, a preference, or it may, if classified as agoraphobia, be a handicap.

Nonetheless, Dworkin makes an exception for someone who has what he terms 'a craving (or obsession or lust ...) that he wishes he did not have'. The examples that Dworkin gives of a person's preferences that may count as cravings are diverse, from 'some feature of his physical needs that other people would not consider a handicap at all: for example, a generous appetite for sex' to those that someone may himself have cultivated, such as 'a taste for a particular sport or for music of a sort difficult to obtain'. What these preferences have in common is that the people who have them 'believe they would be better off without them, but nevertheless find it painful to ignore them'. In Dworkin's view, for such people 'these tastes are handicaps; though for other people they are rather an essential part of what gives value to their lives'.[19]

The concept of a preference that one does not want seems problematic: it certainly sits uncomfortably with Mill's basic principle that 'over himself, over his own body and mind, the individual is sovereign'. (Dworkin appears to recognize this when he says that such a taste is for its possessor 'a "preference" (*if that is the right word*) that he does not want'.[20]) There is also a problem with admitting self-cultivated preferences to the class of handicaps. If you and I start with the same wealth and I squander my wealth but you save yours then I have no claim on your greater wealth. If you and I start with the same wealth and I deliberately develop a taste for polo while you are content to play tennis then it is not clear why I should have a claim on what you have saved by accepting your more modest wants. In each case I am responsible for my actions, and you for yours. Analogous observations would apply to 'cheap tastes', such as those (to use Sen's well-known example) of 'the battered slave, the broken unemployed, the hopeless destitute, [and] the tamed housewife'.[21] If you deal with your destitution by facing up to it and adjusting your life accordingly while I deny mine and fail to make any adjustments then it is not clear why I should have a claim on you.

In summary, whatever definition of handicap is adopted, the survivors (or immigrants, in Dworkin's terminology) amend their auction procedure:

> By way of supplement to the auction, they now establish a hypothetical insurance market which they effectuate through compulsory insurance at a fixed premium for everyone based on speculations about what the average immigrant would have purchased by way of insurance had the antecedent risk of various handicaps been equal.[22]

This process establishes equality of effective resources at the outset, but this equality will typically be disturbed by subsequent economic activity. If some survivors choose to work more than others they will produce, and thus have, more than their more leisurely compatriots. Thus at some stage the envy test will not be met. This, however, does not create a problem because the envy test is to be applied diachronically: 'it requires that no one envy the bundle of occupation and resources at the disposal of anyone else over time, though someone may envy another's bundle at any particular time'.[23] Since everyone had the opportunity to work hard it would, in Dworkin's view, violate rather than endorse equality of resources if the wealth of the hardworking were from time to time to be distributed to the more leisurely.

Again, this point may be expressed more simply in terms of an equal-wealth Walrasian equilibrium where commodities are distinguished by the time at which they are available, so that 'wheat today' and 'wheat tomorrow' are different commodities, and where leisure is also a commodity. However, a problem unavoidably arises if importance is attached to satisfying the envy test for, as noted above, introducing leisure may result in there being no Pareto efficient allocations that meet the test.

The conclusion that wealth should not be periodically redistributed is based on the premise that everyone has the same talents, that is, is equally productive (though there is some ambiguity in Dworkin's treatment as he motivates his discussion with the example of someone who 'was especially proficient at producing tomatoes'.) If people have different talents the picture changes, for in that case 'if we continue to insist that the envy test is a necessary condition of equality of resources, then our initial auction will not insure continuing equality, in the real world of unequal talents for production'.[24]

It might be argued that 'if one person, by dint of superior effort or talent, uses his equal share to create more than another, he is entitled to profit thereby, because his gain is not made at the expense of someone else who does less with his share'. Dworkin rejects this argument on the grounds that it confuses equality of resources with what he sees as being a 'fundamentally different idea sometimes called equality of opportunity'. Dworkin does not say what he means by equality of opportunity, but rejects the argument directly by denying that the gain of the more talented 'is not made at the expense of someone else who does less with his share'.

Dworkin's reason for denying this is that if you are more successful at agriculture than I, then my poor efforts will be rewarded less because people will buy less of my 'inferior produce' and, to add insult to injury, you, being richer, will buy a large amount of wine so that I will be able to drink less. This seems unconvincing, if only because exactly the same outcome might obtain if we had equal talents. If you work more than I do, which Dworkin allows, then you may water your crops more frequently than I do and thus produce more luscious fruit, be richer, and buy more wine; or you could just work the same amount as I do but choose to drink a large amount of wine. (Indeed, Dworkin notes in passing that a similar outcome may arise with equal talents but says that 'the difference ... *if there is one*, lies elsewhere',[25] though where this may be is not indicated.) A more satisfactory approach might be to say that you and I had equal opportunities if we had equal choice sets over commodities (distinguished, as above, by time and state of the world). Then if you had more talents than I, in the sense of being more productive than I am, we would not have equal choice sets and thus not have equal opportunities.

Talents

The essential reason why differential talents create a problem is that equality of resources at the outset will typically be disturbed by subsequent economic activity, not because of morally acceptable differences in work habits, but because of morally arbitrary differences in talents.

Requiring equality of resources only at the outset would be what Dworkin calls a starting-gate theory of fairness, which Dworkin sees as being 'very far from equality of resources' and strongly rejects: 'indeed it is hardly a coherent political theory at all'. Such a theory holds that justice requires equality of initial resources, but accepts laissez-faire thereafter. The fundamental problem with a starting-gate theory is that it relies on some purely arbitrary starting point. In Dworkin's island story the moment when the survivors land on the island is an arbitrary point in their lives at which to insist on equality of resources. If the requirement of equality of resources is to apply at that point then presumably it is to apply on each anniversary of their landing 'which is, in the words of the banal and important cliché, the first day in the rest of their lives',[26] and, indeed, at other arbitrary points. If justice requires a Dworkinian auction when the survivors arrive then it must require such an auction from time to time thereafter; and if justice accepts laissez-faire thereafter, it must accept it when they arrive.

Dworkin requires neither that there be periodic auctions nor that there be laissez-faire at all times. His theory does not suppose that an equal division of resources is appropriate at one point in time but not at any other; it argues only that the resources available to someone at any moment be a function of the resources available to or consumed by him at others. It thus avoids the arbitrariness of any initial position.

A possible way to avoid the problems of the starting-gate theory is for the initial auction to include not only external resources but also the labour of each of the survivors. A survivor would now be able to bid for the right to control parts, or the whole, of his own or anyone else's labour time. If he acquires his own labour time he can work and enjoy the fruits of doing so, or use it for leisure; if he acquires someone else's he can direct that person to work and deliver to him the fruits of this work. Dworkin claims that 'except in unusual cases, since people begin with equal resources for bidding, each agent would bid enough to secure his own labor'. If everyone does this then no one will own a share of anyone else's labour. However, it is not clear what these 'unusual cases' may be, or, more importantly, why someone would acquire all of his, and only his, labour. If he does acquire all of his own labour then, Dworkin claims, in order to pay for it he would either have to spend his life in the most commercially profitable way, or, if he is talented, 'suffer some very serious deprivation'. If you are able to earn a large income as a banker then you will have to spend your days in a bank when, it is supposed, you would rather spend them writing poetry. Others would be prepared to bid a large amount for your labour, and if they acquire it then they will require you to work in the bank; but if you outbid them then you will still have to spend your days in the bank in order to earn enough to pay for your bid. In Dworkin's famous phrase, 'this is indeed the slavery of the talented'.[27] More generally, under this proposal the more talented will typically be worse off than the less talented, and it is primarily for this reason (rather than because of the implied violation of self-ownership rights, which Dworkin dismisses) that Dworkin rejects this proposal in favour of an insurance scheme, to be discussed below. This however, is a mistake, for as Roemer shows, 'the talented can end up *worse off* under a properly specified insurance mechanism than under ... Dworkin's labor auction'.[28]

Dworkin's aim is to specify a scheme that allows the distribution of resources at any point of time to be both ambition-sensitive, in that it reflects the cost or benefit to others of the choices people make, but not be endowment-sensitive, in that it allows scope for differences in ability among people with the same ambitions. It is to 'devise some formula that offers a practical, or even a theoretical, compromise between these two, apparently competing, requirements'. It seeks neither to reward nor penalize talent: 'the principle that people should not be penalized for talent is simply part of the same principle we relied on in rejecting the apparently opposite idea, that people should be allowed to retain the benefits of superior talent'.[29]

To achieve that aim Dworkin considers 'the periodic redistribution of resources through some form of income tax'. An income tax is explicitly preferred to a consumption tax (like Rawls, Dworkin does not recognize that the two are equivalent, apart from timing) or a wealth tax on the grounds that 'someone's decision to spend rather than save what he has earned is precisely the kind of decision whose impact should be determined by the market uncorrected for tax'.[30] Dworkin does not observe that by the same token someone's decision to enjoy leisure rather than consumer goods should also be the kind of decision whose impact should be determined by the market uncorrected for tax, and that a tax on income penalizes the indulgent and rewards the abstemious.

(Dworkin also does not note that an income tax, if it is to lead to a Pareto efficient outcome, may have apparently inegalitarian properties. In particular, it may specify a very low marginal tax rate for high incomes. Assume that under some proposed tax schedule with a marginal rate of 50 per cent, say, for all incomes above $1m the highest earning person has an income of $2m. Now consider the revised tax schedule that is the same as the initial one except that the marginal tax rate for all incomes greater than $2m is 1 per cent. Then the highest earner will typically work more, and be better off, while no one will be worse off. But there will also be some extra tax revenue, from the 1 per cent tax, which may be distributed to everyone equally, making everyone better off. This means that the initial proposed tax schedule, that with a high marginal rate for large incomes, was not Pareto efficient.)

Dworkin recognizes that his tax must effect a compromise, but only a compromise that will 'neutralize the effects of differential talents, yet preserve the consequences of one person choosing an occupation'. Indeed, Dworkin sees the compromise as 'a compromise of two requirements of equality ... not a compromise of equality for the sake of some independent value such as efficiency'. The compromise could be resolved if we were able to identify a component of someone's wealth that originated in his differential talent as distinguished from his differential ambition, but this is not possible: 'we cannot hope to identify such a component, even given perfect information about people's personalities'.[31]

The reason why this component cannot be identified is that ambitions and talents are interrelated, and more inextricably so than are ambitions and handicaps. As Dworkin notes, 'the connection between talents and ambitions ... is much closer than that between ambitions and handicaps'.[32] An ambition may lead to the nurturing and development of talents: if I have the ambition to be an artist I may train and practice accordingly. And a talent may create an ambition: if I discover that I have a natural talent for the piano I may develop the ambition to become a musician. It is because of this close, and reciprocal, interrelationship that Dworkin considers differential talents separately from differential handicaps. If it were not for this difference a talent could simply be seen as a negative handicap or, in more natural language, a handicap as an absence of talent. (On the other hand, it might be argued that ambitions and handicaps are interrelated in the same way as are ambitions and talents, and thus that there is no reason not to see a handicap as an absence of talent. If I have an ambition to be an artist I may undergo surgery to correct my poor sight; and if my hearing is impaired I may abandon my previous ambition to be a pianist.)

To proceed, Dworkin proposes a hypothetical insurance scheme that is analogous to that for handicaps. In this scheme it is supposed that people know what talents they have, but not the income that these will produce, and choose a level of insurance accordingly. Brown[33] criticizes this veil of ignorance construction on the grounds that in order to make an informed choice about insurance people will need to know what goods will be available, and the prices of these. But if people know their talents then they know how much they will be able to produce, and if they know the prices of the goods that are available then they will know the prices of what they will produce, so they know the value of what they will produce, which is their income. However, Dworkin's position may more satisfactorily be understood as involving some exogenous uncertainty. That is, that there are a number of possible states of the world, and earnings may be different in each. I as a talented farmer may earn more if the sun shines than if it does not. Future states of the world are not known: what people are insuring against is the occurrence of adverse states.

Regardless of what individuals know, an imaginary agency knows each person's talents and preferences, and also knows what resources are available and the technology for transforming these into other resources. On the basis of this it computes the income structure, that is, the number of people earning each level of income, that will emerge in a competitive market. Each person may buy insurance from the agency to cover the possibility of his income falling below whatever level he cares to name: one policy will cover him against his income falling below $10,000 per year, another will cover him against this falling below $20,000, and so forth. The premium is not paid in advance, but from the policyholder's future earnings. Dworkin asks 'how much of such insurance would the survivors, on average, buy, at what specified level of income coverage, and at what cost?', and claims that the agency, or computer as he calls it, can answer this question: 'there is no reason to doubt that the computer could furnish an answer'.[34]

This furnishing of an answer raises a dilemma, as Brown has noted. Either it is possible to identify how much of someone's income is due to his talents and how much is due to his preferences, or it is not. If it is possible then this determines whatever redistribution is considered to be appropriate and there is no need for any hypothetical insurance. If it is not possible then 'we cannot know whether the average insured level of income in the hypothetical scenario tracks ambition-sensitivity or endowment-insensitivity'.[35] As Macleod, who also addresses this problem, summarizes the position, 'all told, the problems with Dworkin's approach seem insurmountable', so that 'egalitarians must look elsewhere for a theory of fair market adjustment'.[36]

Even if an answer is furnished, it may be less than satisfactory. Specifically, although Dworkin claims that 'people should not be penalized for talent' they may well be penalized under the hypothetical auction, which may result in the 'slavery of the talented' that Dworkin is eager to avoid. If you have insured yourself against your income being below some high level and it transpires that your income reaches this level then you receive no insurance pay-out, but will need to use your talent as a banker to pay the insurance premium rather than be a poet, which, it is supposed, you would prefer: you would be a slave to your maximum earning power. Dworkin argues that this would not occur, but as Roemer shows, 'appealing as Dworkin's intuition might be, it is incorrect', for it may well be the case that 'a person is more "enslaved" by the insurance agreement if he is born talented'.[37] Further, not only may the more talented be enslaved, but the less talented may be made worse off. Suppose that you and I have the same preferences, but that you have more of every talent than I. Then in every state of the world you will earn more than I, and accordingly, as we have the same preferences (in particular, towards risk), you will purchase less insurance than I do and thus pay a lower premium. This means that in every state of the world you will be unambiguously better off than I am: your income will be higher and your insurance payments lower. More importantly, the difference in our net incomes has been exacerbated by the insurance scheme: it has reduced my net income more than it has reduced yours. This is not because I have different preferences or ambitions: it is simply because I am less talented. As Roemer, from whom this example is derived, notes, 'the example is not an eccentric one: indeed, it is perhaps the central example of inequality of talents'.[38]

Assume, then, that the agency determines the average level of cover that would be chosen in the hypothetical insurance market, together with some appropriate premium. Dworkin then asks, 'can we translate that hypothetical insurance structure into a tax scheme?'. There are a number of reasons why the answer to this question may be that we cannot. One is the moral hazard problem. Eligibility for a payment from the hypothetical insurer, and the level of payment, depend on the insured's highest possible earnings, which are unobservable, rather than on his actual earnings. The insured may thus have an incentive to work in some more congenial but less lucrative occupation: he may prefer to be an artist than to be a miner. Further, he may have an incentive not to develop his earning capacity over time, for example, through education. Dworkin suggests avoiding, or at least reducing, this problem by co-insurance, that is, by phrasing the insurance contract in such a way that the insured meets some part of any claim. But even if this is successful, there will not be universal coverage, which is the aim of the scheme. Dworkin claims that the agency can determine the appropriate amount of co-insurance using only information that it already has, but in fact the agency appears to need more information. To determine the appropriate level of cover and premium when there is no moral hazard the agency need only know each individual's *maximum* earning capacity and his preferences between work and leisure. When there is a possibility of moral hazard the agency needs to know, in addition, *each* possible level of earnings and the insured's preferences between *each* of the occupations associated with these. As Dworkin later accepts, 'policy holders will almost always have more information about their abilities and opportunities than the insurer will'.[39]

This information asymmetry raises a second problem (which Dworkin does not consider). This is the adverse selection problem. Those survivors whose abilities and opportunities are better than those of the average may decline to insure at the average premium. This means that only those whose risk of loss is greater will insure. But the agency, not having this information, will base the premium on the average risk in the population, not on the average risk of those who insure, which is greater. In due course the premium will have to increase, which will deter yet more of those survivors whose risk is relatively low. Eventually, the entire insurance market may collapse, but even if it does not it will, again, fail to provide universal coverage.

Dworkin accepts that 'the actual insurance profile the computer would predict is likely to be much more complex than the simple structure our defective tax system copied';[40] however, he does not indicate how these complexities are to be resolved. Indeed, he goes further, and acknowledges that 'equality of resources is … an indeterminate ideal that accepts, within a certain range, a variety of different distributions'.[41]

Other critics go further still, and argue that however Dworkin's indeterminacy is resolved, equality of resources is incoherent. Roemer considers the spectrum of resource allocation mechanisms that are in some sense resource-equalizing. Precisely what 'equalizing' entails is deliberately left open, but there are four necessary conditions for this. The mechanism should distribute resources in a Pareto efficient way. It must be resource monotonic, in that an increase in the resources available for allocation should not make anyone worse off. It must be symmetric, in that if two people have the same preferences and abilities then they should be allocated the same resources. And it must be consistent, in that it should not damage those whom it seeks to help (as was the case in the example above). Roemer then proves a theorem that shows that, provided utilities cannot be compared, which is Dworkin's position, there is *no* allocation mechanism that satisfies these four necessary conditions, and thus 'that resource egalitarianism is an incoherent notion'.[42]

Alternative approaches

There are similarities between Dworkin's equality of resources theory and Rawls's difference principle theory. Indeed, Dworkin considers that 'the difference principle is an interpretation of equality of resources', and that 'it is impossible to say, a priori, whether the difference principle or equality of resources will work to achieve greater absolute equality'.[43] However, the essential difference between the two approaches is that Dworkin seeks to give a role to personal responsibility, while Rawls does not. In Dworkin's view, justice requires that people be made equal in condition insofar as their condition results from circumstances for which they are not responsible, but treats as acceptable differences in condition that arise from factors for which they are responsible. For example, Dworkin redresses handicaps directly, but Rawls redresses handicaps only if those with handicaps fall into the worst-off class. If there is a fine distinction of classes, or if classes are taken to be individuals, almost all those with handicaps will go without any redress.

Dworkin's approach also shares similarities with Sen's capabilities approach, Arneson's equal opportunity for welfare theory, and Cohen's equal access to advantage theory. But it also differs significantly from each of these in that it does not involve any interpersonal comparisons of utility: as Dworkin makes clear, 'there is no place in the theory … for comparisons of the welfare levels of different people'.[44] In contrast, each of Sen's, Arneson's, and Cohen's theories, as will be seen, do depend on such comparisons, and thus have no application in the context where these comparisons have no meaning.

Equal capabilities

Sen sees the fundamental problem with equality of resources, equality of opportunity for welfare, and equality of access to advantage (as well as with Rawls's theory of justice as fairness) as being that these theories concentrate on means rather than ends. What is important to people, in Sen's view, is not what goods they have, but what capabilities they can enjoy: not whether they have food and transport, but whether they are well-nourished and mobile. The difference arises because people differ in their abilities to convert goods into capabilities: someone with a high metabolic rate may need more food to be well-nourished than someone with a low rate, and someone whose legs are paralyzed may need more transport to be mobile than someone who is able-bodied. Sen interprets justice as requiring that everyone have the same capabilities: 'this type of equality I shall call "basic capability equality"'.[45]

An immediate question which this raises is that of what the relevant capabilities are. Some capabilities are trivial, such as the capability to play tiddlywinks; others are generally perceived as morally bad, such as the capability to inflict torture. Sen does not specify which capabilities are to be considered as relevant, and, indeed, explicitly refuses to defend any 'one predetermined canonical list of capabilities'.[46] However, Nussbaum specifies ten 'central human capabilities', each of which is required to avoid a life being 'so impoverished that it is not worthy of the dignity of a human being',[47] while Vallentyne claims, in effect, that every capability is relevant: 'capabilities are opportunities to function', and 'no matter what the criterion, it is a mistake to hold that there are some functionings (the non-basic ones) the opportunities for which are irrelevant to justice'.[48] In any event, the specification of capabilities must either be arbitrary (except perhaps under Vallentyne's proposal) or favour some conceptions of the good over others.

A second question that capability equality raises is that of how the relevant capabilities, once specified, are to be aggregated, or indexed: such indexation is unavoidable in a theory that requires that I have the same capabilities as you. Sen does not offer any guidance on this, but accepts that 'the problem of indexing the basic capability bundles is a serious one'.[49]

The problems of specifying and aggregating capabilities are analogous to the problems of specifying and aggregating Rawls's primary goods. Accordingly, although not expressed in terms of wellbeing, they necessarily involve interpersonal comparisons. Further, in Sen's approach precise comparisons are required (to establish equality), in contrast with Rawls's, in which comparisons are required only to identify the worst-off.

Equal opportunity for welfare

Arneson considers people planning their lives. Depending on what actions they take today various options will be available to them tomorrow, and so forth:

> We construct a decision tree that gives an individual's possible complete life-histories. We then add up the preference satisfaction expectation for each

possible life history. In doing this we take into account the preferences that people have regarding being confronted with the particular range of options given at each decision point. Equal opportunity for welfare obtains among persons when all of them face equivalent decision trees – the expected value of each person's best (= most prudent) choice of options, second best, ... nth-best is the same.[50]

However, this criterion is incomplete, for 'people might face an equivalent array of options, as above, yet differ in their awareness of these options, their ability to choose reasonably among them, and the strength of character that enables a person to persist in carrying out a chosen option'.[51] People face *effectively* equivalent options if one of three conditions obtains: their options are equivalent and they are equally able to 'negotiate' them; their options are not equivalent but counterbalance their negotiating abilities; or their options are equivalent and any inequalities in their negotiating abilities are due to matters for which they are responsible. Then people have equal opportunity for welfare at some specified time if they each face effectively equivalent options at that time.

If you and I have equal opportunity for welfare today and I behave negligently then you may legitimately have a greater opportunity for welfare tomorrow. People have equal opportunity for welfare in an extended sense if there is some time at which they have equal effective opportunity and any subsequent inequalities are due to their voluntary choices or differentially negligent behaviour. When people have equal opportunity for welfare in the extended sense any actual inequality of welfare is due to factors for which they are responsible. Thus 'any such inequality will be nonproblematic from the standpoint of distributive equality'.[52]

There are a number of problems with this approach, for example, the vagueness of the concepts of awareness of options, of ability to choose reasonably, and of strength of character: indeed, Arneson accepts that 'to some extent it is technically unfeasible or even physically impossible to collect the needed information'.[53] However, the fundamental problem is that the approach requires an interpersonal comparison of utilities: requiring that the 'expected value' of my best choices be the same as that of yours necessarily requires a comparison of my utility with yours.

Equal access to advantage

Cohen sees equal opportunity for welfare as being necessary for justice, but not sufficient: 'welfare' is too narrow a requirement and should be replaced by 'advantage'; and 'opportunity' should be more properly defined as 'access'. Justice then requires equal access to advantage.

Cohen sees advantage as a broader notion than welfare: 'anything which enhances my welfare is *pro tanto* to my advantage, but the converse is not true'.[54] He illustrates the difference by the example of someone whose legs are paralyzed but who is of a preternaturally happy disposition. Under Arneson's equality of opportunity for welfare this unfortunate would, Cohen maintains, have no claim for a wheelchair, but under equality of access to advantage he would: whatever his relative welfare, he is disadvantaged. In addition, this unfortunate is doubly cursed, for although he can move his arms perfectly well, after he has done so he suffers severe pain unless this is removed by his taking an expensive medicine. Cohen maintains that he would have no claim for this medicine under Dworkin's equality of resources either, though still would under equality of access to advantage.

Cohen prefers 'access' to 'opportunity' on the grounds that 'your opportunities are the same whether you are strong and clever or weak and stupid: if you are weak and stupid, you may not use them well – but that implies that you have them'. Deficiencies in such personal characteristics may 'detract from access to valuable things, even if they do not diminish the opportunity to get them'.[55] However, the distinction seems unnecessary in a comparison with equality of opportunity for welfare: Arneson makes the same point in requiring that people face *effectively* equivalent options. In any event, the distinction is essentially semantic.

There are, again, a number of problems with this approach, for example, in the vagueness of the concept of advantage: Cohen 'cannot say, in a pleasingly systematic way, exactly what should count as an advantage … which is surely one of the deepest [questions] in normative philosophy'. He proceeds to note that 'another matter about which I cannot say anything systematic is the problem of how to compare the net advantage positions of different people'.[56] The latter explicitly involves interpersonal comparisons.

Conclusions

The strength of Dworkin's equality of resources theory of justice is that it seeks to introduce ambition-sensitivity without allowing endowment-sensitivity. To the extent to which it succeeds in this it thus, in Cohen's words, incorporates within egalitarianism 'the most powerful idea in the arsenal of the antiegalitarian right: the idea of choice and responsibility'.[57]

However, it is not entirely successful in this endeavour. There are a number of problems with Dworkin's auction scheme, but these may be avoided by adopting its outcome, that of an equal-wealth Walrasian equilibrium, as a specification of justice in its own right, independent of any auction mechanism. The problems with Dworkin's insurance scheme, however, are not so easily avoided: it necessarily damages those whom it seeks to help, or has even less acceptable defects. As Roemer's theorem shows, 'resource egalitarianism is an incoherent notion'. Developments of Dworkin's view, involving equal capabilities, equal opportunity for welfare, or equal access to advantage do not remove this problem, for these all rely on interpersonal comparisons.

In summary, as indicated in Chapter 1, in its aim at least, equality of resources does recognize individual responsibility, but maintains neither full self-ownership nor full resource-ownership.

Notes

1 All references in this chapter that do not specify an author are to Dworkin (1981).
2 Page 285.
3 Section 1.
4 Debreu (1959), chapter 5.
5 Debreu (1959), chapter 6.
6 Page 289.
7 Heath (2004), page 326.
8 Debreu (1959), chapter 6.
9 Varian (1976), section 3.
10 Pazner and Schmeidler (1974), example 1.
11 Page 293.
12 Pages 293–95.
13 Debreu (1959), chapter 7.
14 Page 298.
15 Anderson (1999), page 303.
16 Page 298.
17 Page 301.
18 Arrow (1973), page 254.
19 Pages 302–3, emphasis added.
20 Pages 302–3, emphasis added.
21 Sen (1987), page 11.
22 Page 301.
23 Page 306.
24 Page 307.
25 Pages 307–8, emphasis added.
26 Page 309.
27 Pages 311–12.
28 Roemer (1985), page 171.
29 Pages 311–12.
30 Page 312.
31 Page 313.
32 Page 316.
33 Brown (2009), chapter 3.
34 Page 317.
35 Brown (2009), page 66.
36 Macleod (1998), page 149.
37 Roemer (1985), page 171.
38 Roemer (1996), page 251.
39 Pages 324–26.
40 Page 326.
41 Page 334.
42 Roemer (1985), page 178.
43 Pages 339–41.
44 Page 335.
45 Sen (1980), page 218.
46 Sen (2005), page 158.
47 Nussbaum (2006), pages 76–78.
48 Vallentyne (2005), pages 361–62.
49 Sen (1980), page 219.
50 Arneson (1989), pages 85–86.
51 Arneson (1989), page 86.
52 Arneson (1989), page 86.

53 Arneson (1989), page 87.
54 Cohen (1989), page 916.
55 Cohen (1989), pages 916–17.
56 Cohen (1989), pages 920–920n.
57 Cohen (1989), page 933.

4

ENTITLEMENTS

In the framework in which justice is interpreted as laissez-faire with compensation for morally arbitrary factors, Nozick's[1] entitlements theory (as an extreme) treats no personal attributes as being arbitrary, and thus defines justice simply as laissez-faire, provided that no one's rights are infringed. In this view 'the complete principle of distributive justice would say simply that a distribution is just if everyone is entitled to the holdings they possess under the distribution'.[2]

The basic schema

Nozick introduces his approach to 'distributive justice' by noting that the term is not a neutral one, but presupposes some central authority that is effecting the distribution. But that is misleading, for there is no such body. My property holdings are not allocated to me by some central planner: they arise from the sweat of my brow or through voluntary exchanges with, or gifts from, others. There is 'no more a distributing or distribution of shares than there is a distributing of mates in a society in which persons choose whom they shall marry'.[3] This stance reflects Hayek's position that 'in a free society in which the position of the different individuals and groups is not the result of anybody's design ... differences in rewards simply cannot meaningfully be described as just or unjust'.[4]

Accordingly, Nozick holds that the justice of a state of affairs is a matter of whether individuals are entitled to their holdings. This requires a specification of what being entitled to something entails. In Nozick's schema individuals' entitlements are determined by two principles, justice in acquisition and justice in transfer:

> If the world were wholly just, the following inductive definition would exhaustively cover the subject of justice in holdings.
>
> 1. A person who acquires a holding in accordance with the principle of justice in acquisition is entitled to that holding.

2. A person who acquires a holding in accordance with the principle of justice in transfer, from someone else entitled to the holding, is entitled to the holding.
3. No one is entitled to a holding except by (repeated) applications of 1 and 2.[5]

Nozick's theory emphasizes institutions, or processes, rather than outcomes. It specifies a purely procedural theory of justice, that is, a theory that assesses the justness of a distribution according to the justness of some prior situation (as specified by the principle of justice in acquisition) and of the steps taken in moving from that (as specified by the principle of justice in transfer). The content of these two principles, of justice in acquisition and of justice in transfer, is to be developed, but in essence, acquisition is just if what is acquired is freely available and acquiring it leaves sufficient for others, and transfer is just if it is voluntary.

Davis[6] has noted two apparent problems with this schema. The first is that if I steal an apple from my neighbour and exchange it with you for an orange (to which you are entitled) then I am entitled to the orange, for I have acquired it in accordance with the principle of justice in transfer, that is, by voluntary exchange with you, who, by hypothesis, were entitled to it. The second problem is that if I, being entitled to my present holdings, steal an apple from my neighbour and eat it then the resulting distribution is just for everyone is entitled to the holdings they possess under it: in particular, I possess only things to which I am entitled, for my illegitimately acquired apple no longer exists.

These two apparent problems are, however, only apparent, for Nozick explicitly states that his schema is to apply (only) 'if the world were wholly just', and clearly this does not obtain in either of Davis's two cases, in each of which I have stolen an apple (and, as will be seen, theft is not just). However, all is not entirely clear, for Nozick does not say what he means by 'the world' in his proviso 'if the world were wholly just'. This cannot simply mean 'the distribution', for if it did Nozick's schema would reduce to the unhelpful statement that 'if the world is just then the world is just if X', where X is the condition contained in Nozick's Clauses 1–3. A plausible interpretation of 'if the world were wholly just' would be 'if no one had at any time in the past acquired a holding except by (repeated) applications of Clauses 1 and 2'. If this interpretation is adopted then Davis's two problems vanish.

However, the world may not be wholly just: as Nozick observes, 'not all actual situations are generated in accordance with the two principles of justice in holdings'. The existence of past injustice 'raises the third major topic under justice in holdings: the rectification of injustice in holdings'.[7]

A taxonomy

Nozick proposes a taxonomy of theories of justice with the intention of demonstrating that all theories of justice other than entitlement theories are flawed. The first distinction is that between end-state (or end-result) principles and historical principles. The most obvious examples of end-state principles are current time-slice principles. These 'hold that the justice of a distribution is determined by how things are distributed (who has what) as judged by some structural principle(s) of just distribution'. According to such principles, the justice of a distribution is judged solely on the basis of a matrix specifying each person's holding. Then two distributions are deemed to be equally just if they have the same structures, that is, if the matrices specifying what goods each person holds are the same other than in the labelling of the persons: there is no change in justice if your holdings and my holdings are exchanged. A prime example of a current time-slice principle is that of utilitarianism, which judges between two distributions solely on the basis of the total utility that each generates, and takes no account of your utility compared with mine (assuming, as utilitarianism must, that such a total, and comparison, has any meaning). (Nozick claims that 'welfare economics is the theory of current time-slice principles of justice',[8] but this is misleading: welfare economics is concerned with characterizing Pareto efficiency, which is conspicuously silent on matters of distribution, and thus of justice.)

However, current time-slice principles of justice are not the only end-state principles. A principle that combines time-slice principles from different periods, rather than just looking at the current period, is also an end-state principle. An example of such a principle would be one that assessed the justice of a state of affairs on the basis of a matrix specifying the average of each person's holdings over the last two, or a hundred, days. As Nozick observes, 'a utilitarian or an egalitarian or any mixture of the two over time will inherit the difficulties of his more myopic comrades'; he is not helped by the fact that 'some of the information others consider relevant in assessing a distribution is reflected, unrecoverably, in past matrices'.[9]

Historical principles, in contrast with end-state principles, hold that 'past circumstances or actions of people can create differential entitlements or differential deserts to things'.[10] A principle that says that it is just for a murderer to be incarcerated is an historical principle: in determining whether it is just that he has to suffer the hardships of prison while others enjoy freedom such a principle would look not at the disparities in the freedom of the murderer and others, but at the past actions of each. Similarly, a socialist view that workers deserve the fruits of their labour and that a state of affairs is unjust if it does not reflect this looks at the past actions of workers and of capitalists. It would not accept that a state of affairs in which capitalists receive the whole of the produce was equally as just as the structurally equivalent one in which workers receive the whole of the produce. Historical principles may be entitlement-based or they may be patterned, in the sense to be discussed.

Nozick claims that (a) historical principles are superior to end-state principles, for the reasons suggested above, and (b) of historical principles, patterned principles are deficient, for the reasons to be developed below. However, although Nozick's taxonomy provides a helpful arrangement of theories of justice it is not sufficiently precise for the purpose of demonstrating that all but entitlement theories are flawed. First, the distinction between historical principles and end-state principles is that in the former 'past circumstances *can* create differential entitlements'. There is no requirement that they actually *do*, so that historical principles and end-state principles (or, more precisely, the distributions which these two principles respectively endorse) are not mutually exclusive. Second, within the class of historical principles entitlement-based and patterned principles are not defined in such a way as to be exhaustive, and indeed it is not clear that they are.

Nozick defines a principle of justice to be patterned if 'it specifies that a distribution is to vary along with some natural dimension, weighted sum of natural dimensions, or lexicographic ordering of natural dimensions'; and a distribution is patterned if 'it accords with some patterned principle'. As Nozick accepts, this is a somewhat loose definition for natural dimensions themselves are not defined; in addition 'for any set of holdings some artificial dimensions can be gimmicked up to vary along with the distribution of the set'.[11] Further, a distribution composed from a small (though 'small' is not defined) number of patterned distributions, each operating in different sectors of society (again, not defined, though presumably including wealth, health, and so forth) is to be treated as patterned, as are outcomes generated by combinations of end-state principles. A distribution that is determined by peoples' ages or skin colours, or by their needs or merits, or by any combination of these, is patterned.

Nozick claims that 'almost every suggested principle of distributive justice is patterned'. The entitlement principle, however, is not patterned, for there is no natural dimension, or combination of a 'small' number of natural dimensions, that produces a distribution that it would generate:

> The set of holdings that results when some persons receive their marginal products, others win at gambling, others receive a share of their mate's income, others receive gifts from foundations, others receive interest on loans, others receive gifts from admirers, others receive returns on investment, others make for themselves much of what they have, others find things, and so on, will not be patterned.[12]

Although a distribution generated by the entitlement principle is unpatterned, Nozick accepts that 'heavy strands of patterns will run through it; significant portions of the variance in holdings will be accounted for by pattern-variables'. This is because if, for example, people transfer their holdings to those who value them most then a pattern, of holding according to valuation, will emerge. But it is important to distinguish between the process generating the distribution of holdings and any 'strands of pattern' that may run through the distribution that results from this process. As Nozick expresses it, 'the process whereby the set of holdings is generated will be intelligible, though the set of holdings itself that results from this process will be unpatterned'.[13]

Patterns and liberty

The reason why patterned theories are claimed to be deficient is, simply, that 'liberty upsets patterns.'[14] As Hume expresses it, 'render possessions ever so equal, men's different degrees of art, care, and industry will immediately break that equality'.[15] Nozick argues this using his famous Wilt Chamberlain example. This, however, has potential problems, the main one being that it may assume the property rights that it seeks to justify.

Mr Chamberlain

Suppose that a distribution that is (uniquely) specified as just by some patterned principle of distributive justice is realized: this may be one in which everyone has an equal share of wealth, or where shares vary in any other patterned way. Now there is a basketball player, one Wilt Chamberlain, who is of average wealth but of superior ability. He enters into a contract with his employers under which he will receive 25 cents for each admission ticket sold to see him play. As he is so able a player a million people come to watch him. Accordingly, Mr Chamberlain earns a further $250,000. The question is, is this new distribution, in which Mr Chamberlain is much better off than in the original distribution, and also much better off than the average person, just? One answer must be that it is not, for the new distribution differs from the old, and by hypothesis the old distribution (and only that distribution) was just. On the other hand, the original distribution was just, and people moved from that to the new distribution entirely voluntarily. Mr Chamberlain and his employers voluntarily entered into the contract; all those who chose to buy a ticket to watch Mr Chamberlain play did so voluntarily; and no one else was affected. All holdings under the original distribution were, by hypothesis, just, and people have used them to their advantage: if people were not entitled to use their holdings to their advantage (subject to not harming others) it is not clear why the original distribution would have allocated them any holdings or, indeed, why they could be described as *their* holdings. If the original distribution was just and people voluntarily moved from it to the new distribution then the new distribution must be just.

Because liberty upsets patterns, under any patterned scheme 'capitalist acts between consenting adults' would have to be forbidden and there would have to be 'continuous interference with people's lives'.[16] As Hume puts it, 'the most rigorous inquisition too is requisite to watch every inequality on its first appearance; and the most severe jurisdiction, to punish and redress it'; indeed, 'so much authority must soon degenerate into tyranny'.[17] Nozick accepts that 'it puts things perhaps a bit too strongly to say that every patterned (or end-state) principle is liable to be thwarted by the voluntary actions of the individual parties transferring some of their shares they receive under the principle', for 'perhaps some *very* weak patterns are not so thwarted'.[18] However, he does not specify the nature of these weak patterns.

The Chamberlain argument may be interpreted, though Nozick does not express it in these terms (other than in a footnote concerning gifts[19]), as claiming that if one distribution is just and a second distribution is Pareto superior to it then that second distribution is just. Nozick asks, 'if $D1$ was a just distribution, and people voluntarily moved from it to D2, transferring parts of their shares they were given under D1 ... isn't D2 also just?'.[20] If everyone voluntarily exchanged their holdings under D1 for those under D2 then they would have chosen D2 over D1, which means that they preferred D2 to D1, which in turn means that D2 is Pareto superior to D1. Thus a Pareto improvement does not infringe justice.

Nozick seeks to draws on Sen's view that 'in a very basic sense liberal values conflict with the Pareto principle'[21] to support his position: 'Sen's argument leads us again to the result that patterning requires continuous interference with individuals' actions and choices'.[22] The basic idea is that imposing even a Pareto efficient pattern will violate people's liberal rights. However, it is not clear that Sen's theorem, which shows that there is no acceptable social choice rule that is consistent with the Pareto criterion and even the most minimal liberalism (together with some technical conditions) supports Nozick's view. Sen's result concerns social choice mechanisms while Nozick's concerns justice, and although each can inform the other, results in one domain cannot directly be applied to the other.

In the Chamberlain example the second distribution is claimed to be Pareto superior to the first because, as has been seen, some have benefited by the move and none have lost. Nozick claims that 'after someone transfers something to Wilt Chamberlain, third parties *still* have their legitimate shares; *their* shares are not changed'. But this may not be the case. If I do not pay to watch Mr Chamberlain play then my share is unchanged, but I may still be worse off. I may feel unhappy about living in a society in which someone has $250,000, or I may simply be envious of Mr Chamberlain's wealth. If that is the case then I am worse off in the second distribution: the second distribution is not Pareto superior to the first. Nozick acknowledges this problem when he asks 'might not a transfer have instrumental effects on a third party, changing his feasible options?', and notes that 'it also might be objected that the transfer might make a third party more envious because it worsens his position relative to someone else'.[23] However, he finds 'it incomprehensible how this can be thought to involve a claim of justice', though develops no argument in support of this dismissal of the problem.

Cohen seeks to make a similar point by claiming that 'Nozick tacitly supposes that a person willing to pay twenty-five cents to watch Wilt play, is *ipso facto* a person willing to pay *Wilt* twenty-five cents to watch him play', and that this supposition is false. There is a difference between a world in which a million people pay 25 cents each to watch Mr Chamberlain play, and a world in which they do that and in addition Mr Chamberlain is $250,000 the richer. Cohen claims that the problem with the latter world arises because the value of a person's share depends on what he can do with it, and that in turn depends in part on what others have. For example 'the Chamberlain fans, acting independently, are less likely than Chamberlain is to buy a set of houses and leave them unoccupied, with speculative intent'.[24] This example seems misplaced, for if Mr Chamberlain sees the houses as a good speculation it is not clear why his fans would not also see this (and join together contributing a further 25 cents each if necessary). But that aside, we must assume that each fan knew that he was paying his 25 cents to Mr Chamberlain: if he was told otherwise then the transaction would have been fraudulent and thus not voluntary.

There remains a coordination problem. Each person individually may be content to move from one distribution to another but they may all be worse off as a result. I may pay 25 cents for my ticket but find that when I have done so and many others have done the same I have to sit in great discomfort and see nothing. This is an example of Hardin's[25] Tragedy of the Commons (the tendency of individuals' optimal use of a resource to exceed the optimal social use of the resource). This problem is, however, orthogonal to the Chamberlain example.

Independently of the Chamberlain example Nozick illustrates the 'continual interference' and implied restriction of liberty involved in maintaining a pattern with his claim that the 'taxation of earnings from labor is on a par with forced labor', although he is 'unsure' whether 'on a par with' means 'is one kind of', or just 'similar to'. Nozick's aim is to demonstrate that if forced labour is unacceptable then so is the taxation of earnings. As Nozick sees it, 'taking the earnings of n hours labor is like taking n hours from the person; it is like forcing the person to work n hours for another's purpose'. Even if this is not accepted, though 'some persons find this claim obviously true', it is claimed that anyone who does object to forced labour must 'oppose forcing unemployed hippies to work for the benefit of the needy'; they must also 'object to forcing each person to work five extra hours each week for the benefit of the needy'.[26]

A tax on earnings may make me work more or less. On the one hand, the tax has made me poorer so I typically consume less of things, and in particular, less leisure; that is, I work more. On the other hand, the tax has made leisure relatively cheaper: if my wage is $100 per hour then an hour of leisure costs me $100 when there is no tax but only $50 when there is a 50 per cent tax. Accordingly, I consume more leisure, that is, I work less. If the second effect dominates the first, that is, if the tax acts as a disincentive (as is often claimed) then taxation on earnings is on a par with forced leisure, not forced labour.

The essence of Nozick's argument is that 'the fact that others intentionally intervene, in violation of a side constraint against aggression, to threaten force to limit the alternatives, in this case to paying taxes or (presumably the worse alternative) bare subsistence, makes the taxation system one of forced labor'.[27] However, any tax system backed by the power of the state, as all must be, necessarily threatens force to limit alternatives, as indeed does any form of state intervention, so that this observation is of little relevance.

Nozick also observes that a tax on earnings affects some people more than others, and asks why a person who 'prefers seeing a movie (and who has to earn money for a ticket) be open to the required call to aid the needy, while the person who prefers looking at a sunset (and hence need earn no extra money) is not?'.[28] (As an aside, he finds it surprising that someone who can so easily obtain pleasure is let off lightly while the unfortunate who must work for his pleasures is further burdened.) This observation adds little. Any tax system limits people's options, and thus (other than in trivial cases) affects their behaviour: some of the options they may have chosen are no longer available to them. And any tax system that affects people's behaviour necessarily burdens some more than others (unless, trivially, all people are identical).

Property rights

The main problem with the Chamberlain argument is not that concerning third parties or forced labour, but that it assumes the property rights that it seeks to justify. As O'Neill puts it, 'the argument presupposes, so does not demonstrate, that it is wrong to interfere to restore disturbed patterns or end-states, and that such restorations ... violate individuals' property rights'. But 'it is just these property rights which have yet to be established'. Thus 'the interpretation of property rights must be established before the restoration of patterns ... can be rejected'.[29] The Chamberlain example assumes that individual property rights are rights to do what one will with one's property (subject to the rights of others), and in particular to dispose of it in any way that one sees fit. However, the legitimacy of property rights must be established before the restoration of patterns can be said to constitute an '*unwarranted* interference with peoples' lives'. Nozick is correct in stating that a socialist society would have to forbid 'capitalist acts between consenting adults', but this would only be an unwarranted interference if people had full capitalist rights to start with. That they do is a claim that must be established by independent means. This view underlies Fried's claim that 'it is not clear that Nozick has any theory of property rights at all'.[30]

Ryan seeks to illustrate this point with the example of university teaching positions in philosophy, which, he claims, are held according to some patterned principle, such as merit or teaching ability. If individuals were free to sell their positions then the pattern would be disturbed, but individuals are not free to sell them. Ryan asks whether we should 'conclude that the personal liberty of those who hold positions is infringed upon, or restricted, because they cannot *sell* their jobs'. We would not, he answers, for 'this would be absurd'. Accordingly, forbidding capitalist acts between consenting adults does not necessarily infringe their personal liberty. However, Ryan's example is not convincing. Teaching positions are not 'holdings' in Nozick's sense, despite the linguistic usage of 'holding a job'. A position is not property, it is a contractual arrangement. The fact that a contract between you and me imposes certain obligations on each of us says nothing about whether my being restricted from exchanging my property with you infringes our liberty. Nonetheless, despite the unconvincing nature of Ryan's example the underlying problem remains: the Chamberlain argument assumes the type of property rights that it seeks to justify, or, as Ryan correctly generalizes from his flawed example, 'what Nozick tries to show is that personal *liberty* upsets patterns: not private property rights, but personal liberty requires that we adopt an entitlement conception of justice'.[31]

Nozick states that 'there is *no* question about whether each of the people was entitled to the control over the resources they held in $D1$',[32] the assumed just distribution. But that must depend on what is meant by 'control': it is only the case if my having control over something implies that I have full property rights in that thing, and in particular the right to alienate it, which is what the Chamberlain example is meant to demonstrate. For example, a Marxist could, without any inconsistency, claim that the rights of ownership extend only to personal items and not to the means of production. Individuals would have the right to use the latter in various ways, but not to sell them. Or, as Nagel argues, the 'absolute entitlement to property is not what would be allocated to people under a partially egalitarian distribution'; rather, 'possession would confer the kind of qualified entitlement that exists under a system in which taxes and other conditions are arranged to preserve certain features of the distribution'.[33] Then simply because an individual received a holding in the original distribution it would not follow that he was entitled to alienate it, as those who paid to watch Mr Chamberlain did with their 25 cents. Indeed, Nozick himself, as will be seen, uses the Lockean proviso to restrict the alienation of certain property. As Ryan concludes, 'Nozick's is not really a case against patterned distributions of "holdings" in general – it is at best a case against patterned distributions of privately owned property'.[34]

Self-ownership

As Vallentyne points out, a 'puzzling feature of this [Nozick's] schema is that it makes no mention of the *initial rights* that individuals may have prior to acquisition and transfer', but 'a very natural thought is that individuals typically have certain rights over their bodies'.[35] An obvious way to remedy that deficiency is by introducing a principle of self-ownership.

Self-ownership in this context is to be understood in what Vallentyne calls the political, as opposed to the moral, sense. The former concerns 'the *legitimately enforceable* moral rights correlative to the legitimately enforceable moral duties of others', whereas the latter 'concerns the moral rights correlative to the moral duties of others'.[36] The political sense is stronger than the moral in that it asserts that self-ownership rights are legitimately enforceable, but is weaker in that it does not rule out having unenforceable moral ties to others.

Although Nozick mentions self-ownership only once (when discussing taxation[37]) this concept underlies his theory: as Cohen notes 'the primary commitment of his [Nozick's] philosophy is … to the thesis of self-ownership'.[38] The way in which Nozick expresses this commitment is in terms of side constraints: 'side constraints upon action reflect the underlying Kantian principle that individuals are ends and not merely means; they may not be sacrificed or used for the achieving of other ends without their consent'; thus 'individuals are inviolable'. The nature of side constraints is developed further as follows:

> The moral side constraints upon what we may do, I claim, reflect the fact of our separate existences. They reflect the fact that no moral balancing act can take place among us; there is no moral outweighing of one of our lives by

others so as to lead to a greater overall social good. There is no justified sacrifice of some of us for others. This root idea, namely, that there are different individuals with separate lives and so no one may be sacrificed for others, underlies the existence of moral side constraints, but it also, I believe, leads to a libertarian side constraint that prohibits aggression against another.[39]

Nozick's commitment to self-ownership is an aspect of his emphasis on rights. As has been noted, Nozick starts with the premise that 'individuals have rights, and there are things no person or group may do to them (without violating their rights)'. But these rights are not absolute: as Nozick acknowledges, 'my property rights in my knife allow me to leave it where I will, but not in your chest'.[40] In this he reflects Locke's distinction between liberty and licence: 'though this [the state of nature] be a *state of liberty*, yet it is *not a state of licence*',[41] which is to say that I am not free to do whatever I want, only what is consistent with the rights of others.

The principle of self-ownership has its origins in the Kantian formula for moral equality, that is, in treating people as ends in themselves. It is given a more explicit formulation by Locke who asserts that 'every man has a *property* in his own *person*'; and 'this no body has any right to but himself'.[42] Accordingly, 'the *labour* of his body, and the *work* of his hands, we may say, are properly his'. The principle is developed by a number of nineteenth-century writers: it is put most succinctly by Walras in a definition, two lemmata, his first theorem, and his explication of that theorem:

Definition A person's property in a thing is the person's right to apply the thing in satisfaction of a need, even by consuming it.
Lemma I The owner of a thing is the owner of the services produced by it.
Lemma II The owner of a thing is the owner of the price of it.
Theorem I Personal faculties are, by natural law, the property of the individual.

In other words, each person owns himself, because each person, that is, each rational and free creature, has the right and duty to pursue his own ends and achieve his destiny, and is responsible for this pursuit and achievement. Here, the principle of inequality applies, which requires that we benefit in proportion to our efforts. ... The individual, being the owner of his personal faculties, will be the owner of his labour (Lemma I) and of his salary, as well as of the products, consumption, or investments acquired by him with his salary (Lemma II).[43]

A standard modern statement of the principle, that provided by Cohen, is that 'each person enjoys, over herself and her powers, full and exclusive rights of control and use, and therefore owes no service or product to anyone else that she has not contracted to supply'.[44] I have full ownership of myself if, as Cohen expresses it, I have all the legal rights that someone has over a slave:

> Each person possesses over himself, as a matter of moral right, all those rights that a slaveholder has over a complete chattel slave as a matter of legal right, and he is entitled, morally speaking, to dispose over himself in the way such a slaveholder is entitled, legally speaking, to dispose over his slave.[45]

Since a slaveholder has the legal rights to the labour of his slave and the fruits of that labour, each person is the morally rightful owner of his labour and of the fruits thereof. As Cohen continues, 'the term "self" in the name of the thesis of self-ownership has a purely reflexive significance': it 'signifies that what owns and what is owned are one and the same, namely, the whole person'. Accordingly, there is 'no need to establish that my arm or my power to play basketball well is a proper part of my self, in order for me to claim sovereignty over it under the thesis of self-ownership'.[46]

An intuitive argument in favour of self-ownership is suggested by Wolff's eye lottery. In this example it is supposed that eyes may be transplanted without any problems. As some people are born with defective eyes the possibility of redistributing eyes arises. 'Should we', asks Wolff, 'have a national lottery, and force the losers to donate an eye?' 'This seems monstrous', Wolff continues, even though 'it would be a better world, of course, if everyone could see, but does this justify holding the eyeball lottery and redistributing eyes?'.[47]

Cohen argues that this example is not convincing. He considers a different example, in which no one is born with good eyes but the state implants perfect artificial eyes perinatally. However, sometimes people lose an eye, and the only way to restore their sight is to remove an eye from someone else, for new artificial eyes cannot be implanted into adults. Cohen suggests that we may not feel that this possibility is as 'monstrous', and claims that if we do not then 'the suggestion arises that our resistance to a lottery for natural eyes shows not belief in self-ownership but hostility to severe interference in someone's life'. For example, 'the state need never vest ownership of the eyes in persons: they could be regarded as on loan, with one of them being retrievable if your number comes up in a lottery'. Cohen adds that it is the involuntary nature of the use of someone's body parts that is at issue, rather than simply that they are body parts: people 'can condemn rape (the violent borrowing of sexual organs) while also condemning prostitution (the peaceful hiring out of same)'.[48]

It has been claimed, for example by Taylor,[49] using an argument based on Kant's third formulation of the categorical imperative, that self-ownership is entailed by the principle of autonomy, that is, that one should be able to determine one's life within a morally permissible range of choices. However, self-ownership does not ensure autonomy, for at least two reasons. First, if I am poor then universal self-ownership may give me less autonomy than a scheme of universal partial self-ownership under which everyone has a duty to assist the poor. Second, self-ownership is a purely formal notion, and does not ensure effective autonomy: if the external world is owned by others then I can effect no physical action without someone else's approval, since anything I do would involve using someone else's property. It might further be argued that even if everyone had the same wealth, full self-ownership may provide less autonomy than a scheme of universal partial self-ownership that provides public goods such as a legal system that protects the right of self-ownership itself. This is echoed by Arneson in his observation that self-ownership in some circumstances 'conflicts with Pareto optimality, a very minimal requirement of fairness'.[50] However, this further point to some extent begs the question: if everyone respects others' self-ownership there is no need for such goods.

Nozick considers that 'the central core of the notion of a property right in X, relative to which other parts of the notion are to be explained, is the right to determine what shall be done with X', so that someone having ownership of himself would involve his 'having a right to decide what would become of himself and what he would do, and as having a right to reap the benefits of what he did'.[51]

Nozick's remarks are developed by Otsuka, who defines a person to be a (full) self-owner if he 'possesses, to the greatest extent and stringency compatible with the same possession by others, the aforementioned rights "to decide what would become of himself and what he would do, and … reap the benefits of what he did"'.[52] However, Otsuka sees this as involving an unresolvable dilemma. Self-ownership must either be compatible with incursions upon one's body that result in harm, or incompatible with these. If it is compatible then it is not clear why you cannot force me (perhaps under threat of what would then be legitimate bodily harm) to work for you. If it is incompatible then, in Sandel's[53] trolley-car example, one may not turn a trolley-car that will otherwise run over five people on to a side track where it will instead run over a sixth. Nozick does not address this dilemma explicitly, but it is clear that he would endorse the incompatibility alternative: he asks 'why may not one violate persons for the greater social good?', and provides the answer that 'to use a person in this way does not sufficiently respect and take account of the fact that he is a separate person'.[54]

Rothbard proposes a justification of the rights of self-ownership, which he interprets as 'the absolute right of each man, by virtue of his (or her) being a human being, to "own" his or her own body; that is, to control that body free of coercive interference'. This justification asserts that if self-ownership is denied then either (a) one class of people has the right to own another class, or (b) everyone has the right to own an equal share of everyone else. The first alternative, it is claimed, implies that the second class 'is in reality subhuman', but since its members are by hypothesis people and thus human there is a contradiction. The second alternative 'rests on an absurdity: proclaiming that every man is entitled to own a part of everyone else, yet is not entitled to own himself'.[55] However, it is not clear that (a) and (b) exhaust the possibilities of the denial of self-ownership: each person could own a part of, say, his immediate neighbour. Further, in (a) your having part-ownership of me does not make me subhuman. And in (b) communal ownership, which is what is implied, has its problems but is not logically 'absurd': it would be logically absurd for you to own all of me and for I to own all of you, but there is no logical problem in your owning a tenth, say, of me and my owning a tenth of you.

Nonetheless, Rothbard concludes that the 'primary axiom [of liberty is] the universal right of self-ownership, a right held by everyone by virtue of being a human being'.[56] In this he echoes Arneson, who claims that 'the principle is foundational for one tradition of political liberalism running from Locke to Nozick',[57] and Narveson, who holds that 'the libertarian thesis is really the thesis that *a right to our own persons as our property is the sole fundamental right there is*'.[58]

Justice in acquisition

The essence of Nozick's principle of justice in acquisition is that acquisition is just if what is acquired is freely available and acquiring it leaves sufficient for others. Giving an operational meaning to this requires the specification of what acquisition means, what is freely available, and how leaving sufficient for others is to be interpreted. In doing this, Nozick, albeit with reservations, follows Locke:

> Whatsoever then he removes out of the state that nature hath provided, and left it in, he hath mixed his *labour* with, and joined to it something that is his own, and thereby makes it his *property*. It being by him removed from the common state nature hath placed it in, it hath by this *labour* something annexed to it, that excludes the common right of other men: for this *labour* being the unquestionable property of the labourer, no man but he can have a right to what that is once joyned to, at least where there is enough, and as good left in common for others.[59]

Acquisition

Locke, then, interprets 'acquiring' as 'mixing one's labour with'. I own my labour, and if I inextricably mix my labour with something that no one else owns then I make that thing my own. If I plough a previously unowned plot of land then I have mixed my labour with that land, and it becomes mine. However, as Nozick points out (without proposing any resolution of these) there are a number of problems with this interpretation.

First, it is not clear why mixing something that I own with something that I do not own implies that I gain the latter rather than lose the former. In Nozick's example, 'if I own a can of tomato juice and spill it in the sea ... do I thereby come to own the sea, or have I foolishly dissipated my tomato juice?'. Avoiding each extreme, it might be more plausible if I were entitled only to the added value that my labour had achieved, rather then to the whole object: if I were entitled to the increase in the value of the land that I had ploughed, rather than to the land itself. Operationally, however, this may not be very helpful: as Nozick claims, though without argument, 'no workable or coherent value-added property scheme has yet been devised'. Second, it is not clear what determines how much of the unowned resource I come to own. If I build a fence around a previously unowned plot of land do I own all that I have enclosed, or simply the land under the fence? In Nozick's example, 'if a private astronaut clears a place on Mars, has he mixed his labor with (so that he comes to own) the whole planet, the whole uninhabited universe, or just a particular plot?'.[60]

An alternative interpretation of acquiring, and one that avoids the obscurity involved in the concept of mixing one's labour, is that of discovering. If I discover and lay claim to an uninhabited and previously undiscovered island then it becomes mine. As Kirzner expresses it,

> Until a resource has been discovered, *it has not*, in the sense relevant to the rights of access and common use, *existed at all*. On this view it seems plausible to consider the discoverer (of the hitherto 'non-existent' resource) as, in the relevant sense the *creator* of what he has found.[61]

Accordingly, the creator is entitled to that which he has created. This form of acquisition is not the same as acquisition from nature. The latter occurs against a background of given and known resources: it may be seen as a form of transfer, from nature to the first owner. The former involves no form of transfer: there is no resource to transfer until it is discovered/created.

Acquisition by discovery may also be construed as applying even where everyone other than the acquirer knew of the resource (so that there is no 'discovery') but did not think it worth their while to appropriate it. If everyone knew that there were pearl-bearing oysters on the sea-bed but you were the only one prepared to dive for them, then you may plausibly be said to be entitled to the oysters that you recover and the pearls that they contain.

Laurence Sterne, who is much influenced by Locke (though does not share Locke's preference for judgement over wit), makes the Lockean argument somewhat more forcefully in *Tristram Shandy* when John picks up an opinion 'as a man in a state of nature picks up an apple – it becomes his own'. But does it, he asks?

> Whence comes this man's right to this apple? ex confesso, he will say – things were in a state of nature – The apple, is as much Frank's apple as John's. Pray, Mr. Shandy, what patent has he to shew for it? and how did it begin to be his? was it, when he set his heart upon it? or when he gathered it? or when he chew'd it? or when he roasted it? or when he peel'd, or when he brought it home? or when he digested? – or when he – ? – For 'tis plain, Sir, if the first picking up of the apple, made it not his – that no subsequent act could.[62]

It does, is the answer:

> The sweat of a man's brows, and the exudations of a man's brains, are as much a man's own property as the breeches upon his backside; – which said

exudations, &c. being dropp'd upon the said apple by the labour of finding it, and picking it up; and being moreover indissolubly wasted, and as indissolubly annex'd, by the picker up, to the thing pick'd up, carried home, roasted, peel'd, eaten, digested, and so on; – 'tis evident that the gatherer of the apple, in so doing, has mix'd up something which was his own, with the apple which was not his own, by which means he has acquired a property; – or, in other words, the apple is John's apple.[63]

Freely available

Locke interprets 'freely available' as being 'in the state that nature hath provided', and Nozick (without any argument) follows Locke in equating 'freely available' with 'unowned'. There are however, other possibilities. Virgin resources may be seen as being owned in common, or as being jointly owned in equal shares. Under common ownership anyone may use, but not appropriate, them; under joint ownership any use, and any appropriation, requires universal consent. The essential reason why appropriation requires this is that, as Gibbard expresses it, 'to appropriate is not to commit an act that changes the physical world; it is to alter the rights of others'.[64] Accordingly, those others must give their consent to have their rights so altered. Herein lies a problem, for it may be that obtaining universal consent is impractical, at least in large societies. In that case any viable form of communal ownership will need to be unilateralist, in the sense that people are permitted to use resources without obtaining universal consent, and also to appropriate them subject to some universally agreed compensation rule, it being more plausible that some such rule is universally agreed than that each individual appropriation is.

If universal approval is required then each person will give his consent to some appropriation only if the resulting scheme of ownership is to his benefit, so the scheme that emerges will be the result of a process of bargaining. As Gibbard[65] shows, if all bargainers are alike, and the resource is reasonably plentiful, the efficient symmetrical bargaining outcome would allow each person to appropriate freely, with no side payments. The outcome is thus the same as if no approval were required under a pure Lockean process. However, if people are not alike, the position changes. If some people are handicapped they do not stand to gain much from a system of private ownership: those who do stand to gain will need to offer the handicapped some side payments, or compensation, to obtain their consent. The outcome now is closer to a welfare state.

Leaving sufficient

As has been seen, Locke interprets leaving sufficient for others as there being 'enough, and as good, left in common for others'; this is the famous Lockean proviso. Nozick accepts the need for a proviso on these lines, for if someone appropriates some land then this may make others worse off: before the appropriation they were able to use the land, now they are not. However, it may be that others are not worse off. In Nozick's example, 'if I appropriate a grain of sand from Coney Island, no one else may now do as they will with that grain of sand'; however, 'there are plenty of other grains of sand left for them to do the same with'.[66] Indeed, my appropriation may make others better off: if I appropriate a common then the Tragedy of the Commons is avoided (even if I have benefited far more than anyone else). Or, to use Cohen's example,[67] assume that I enclose a beach that has been common land and enhance its value, for example, by picking up litter every night, and then charge everyone who uses it an admission fee. It may well be that all potential users prefer to use the beach as it now is at the cost of the admission fee than to use it as it was for no fee. If that is the case then my appropriation (or, more precisely, the litter collection which is made viable by my appropriation) has again made everyone better off.

A potential problem with the Lockean proviso is that, as Nozick shows by his 'zip back' line of reasoning, 'there appears to be an argument for the conclusion that if the proviso no longer holds, then it cannot ever have held'.[68] This problem is, in essence, the same as Gibbard's problem. Gibbard[69] considers the case where there was in 1776, say, an abundance of land in some locality, but by 2000 all land in the locality has been appropriated. To resolve the question of whether an appropriation in 1776 is permissible Gibbard treats land as a dated commodity: the commodity 'a plot of land' comprises a number of parts: 'the plot for the year 1776 only', 'the plot for the year 1777 only', and so forth. The right to appropriate the plot for 1776 does not imply the right to appropriate the plot for 1777, or for 2000.

Nozick seeks to avoid this problem in a different way, by distinguishing between a strict and a weak version of the Lockean proviso. I may be made worse off by your appropriating a particular plot of land in two ways: by no longer being able to appropriate it myself, and by no longer being able to use it. The strict version of the proviso requires that I not be made worse off in either of these ways; the weak version requires only that I not be made worse off in the second way. Nozick adopts the weak version:

> Any adequate theory of justice in acquisition will contain a proviso similar to the weaker of the ones we have attributed to Locke. A process normally giving rise to a permanent bequeathable property right in a previously unowned thing will not do so if the position of others no longer at liberty to use the thing is thereby worsened.[70]

The question of what is meant by 'enough, and as good' in the Lockean proviso seems unproblematic in the grain of sand case, but is not as clear in more interesting cases. Steiner,[71] in what has been called equal share libertarianism, interprets 'leaving enough, and as good' as meaning leaving an equally valuable share. This, however, requires that market value be placed on resources, which raises its own problems, though ones which may, as Steiner argues elsewhere,[72] be overcome by a Dworkinian-style auction.

Otsuka proposes a more subjective interpretation, in what has been called opportunity for wellbeing libertarianism. This formulation interprets 'leaving enough, and as good' as meaning leaving an equally good share, in the following sense:

> Someone else's share is as good as yours if and only if it is such that she would be able (by producing, consuming, and trading) to better herself to the same degree as you, where 'betterment' is to be measured in terms of increases in welfare. The phrase 'to the same degree' can be interpreted either as (1) 'by the same increment of increase in welfare' or (2) 'to the same absolute level of welfare'.[73]

The intention behind this specification is that 'those who are, through no fault of theirs, less able to convert worldly resources into welfare are entitled to acquire additional resources in order to compensate for this lesser ability'.[74] While Steiner's interpretation suffers from the problems associated with objective valuation, Otsuka's suffers from the far more serious ones of subjective valuation. The assessment of 'the same absolute level of welfare' requires interpersonal comparisons of utility; and the assessment of 'the same increment of increase in welfare' requires both that and some form of cardinal utility. As was noted in Chapter 1, each of these is without meaning in the absence of some imposed conception of the good.

'The crucial point', as Nozick emphasizes, 'is whether appropriation of an unowned object worsens the situation of others'.[75] The question is, then, what constitutes 'worsening'? Nozick interprets this solely in material terms, but there are other considerations. As noted above, if I appropriate a common then the Tragedy of the Commons is avoided and everyone may be better off in material terms. However, other people may suffer a reduction in autonomy, for if they are not to starve the only practical course of life that remains open to them is working for me as agricultural labourers (and even this depends on my agreeing to employ them). Since Nozick places a high value on the freedom to lead our lives in accordance with our own conception of the good it appears inconsistent to interpret being worse off only in a material way, ignoring any loss of autonomy. Further, as Otsuka[76] notes, my labourers, having to work all day for me, would be preempted from making any acquisitions of their own that would improve their situation.

There is also a worsening in a sense that reflects Bentham's position that my ownership of some thing necessarily prevents others doing what they will with that thing: 'how is your house made yours?', he asks. 'By debarring every one else from the liberty of entering it without your leave',[77] is his answer. If I appropriate a plot of land I take away the liberty that you previously had of walking on the land: I impose on you a new obligation, that of non-interference, and thus make you worse off. Indeed, it has been claimed that the Lockean proviso does not just permit worsening in this way, but places logically impossible burdens on those whose lot is worsened. As Steiner expresses it,

Any such theory is *strictly incoherent*. It is incoherent because, by thus empowering a subset of self-owning persons unilaterally to acquire unencumbered ownership of *all* natural resources, it implies that, in the absence of those owners' permission, later arrivals are encumbered with *unperformable duties* of non-trespass, the enforcement of which unavoidably violates those later arrivals' self-ownership rights.[78]

A further problem concerns the specification of the base line, that is, being worse off than under what? Nozick interprets the Lockean proviso as allowing me to appropriate land if by so doing I do not make others worse off than they would have been had the land remained unowned. This, however, ignores other possibilities, such as your appropriating the land, or our appropriating it jointly. It is, in effect, a first-come, first-served doctrine of appropriation. But it is not clear why this should be seen as more just than a system under which everyone had an equal chance to appropriate. An alternative interpretation of your being harmed would be your being worse off than you would have been under any other scheme of using the land, not just than had the land remained unowned. This, however, is a strong requirement.

As Cohen emphasizes, the only counterfactual that Nozick considers is that in which the land remained available to all. But as Cohen shows by a lengthy example,[79] there are other intuitively relevant counterfactuals compared with which people would be substantially worse off, even if they were better off than had the resource remained available to all. Indeed, Cohen claims that 'there will always be some who would have been better off under an alternative dispensation that it would be arbitrary to exclude from consideration', citing as an example of such a dispensation 'that whose rule is that everyone must slave for the tallest person in society'. He concludes that 'one must therefore abandon the Lockean way of assessing the legitimacy of economic systems'.[80]

A similar conclusion is reached by Steiner, who notes that if I had appropriated the land then I have deprived X of the right to it, and also deprived Y and Z (amongst others) of the right to it, but that only one of these could have appropriated it instead of me. If X appropriated the land this would have deprived me, Y, and Z of the right to it, and so forth. Steiner concludes that 'the resulting vicious circularity renders the impositions of the compensation proviso – and thus, the meaning of Nozick's appropriative right – entirely indeterminable'.[81]

The question of leaving sufficient applies to acquisition from nature only: in acquisition by discovery the Lockean proviso does not apply. If I discover/create a resource then no one is worse off as a result. Nozick implicitly accepts this position: if 'someone finds a new substance in an out-of-the-way place' then 'he does not worsen the situation of others; if he did not stumble upon the substance no one else would have, and the others would remain without it'.[82] There is, however, a problem if as time goes by it becomes more likely that others would have come across it, so that someone's owning the total supply may eventually make others worse off. Nozick accepts that this is a grey area, but makes no proposal as to how to deal with it, other than to suggest that the original acquirer's rights to bequeath the supply of the substance be limited.

The Lockean proviso tests the legitimacy of a holding that has been acquired from nature by determining whether anyone would have been worse off had the acquisition not been made, that is, by looking at the end result. Accordingly, the question arises as to whether this proviso turns Nozick's entitlement principle into an end-state principle. Kuflik claims that it does: 'to make his theory plausible, Nozick introduces a consideration that he calls "the Lockean proviso"' and 'in so doing introduces an "end-state" constraint of his own'.[83] However, it may be argued that the proviso merely refines the principles of acquisition and transfer. The proviso may indeed constrain the outcome of those principles, but only does so indirectly, by virtue of these refinements. This is Nozick's view: as he makes clear when showing that the proviso does not apply in the case of someone finding a new substance, 'the Lockean proviso is not an "end-state principle"; it focuses on a particular way that appropriative actions affect others, and not on the structure of the situation that results'.[84]

Justice in transfer

As has been noted, the essence of Nozick's principle of justice in transfer is that a transfer is just if it is voluntary, in that each party consents to it. This consent must be explicit: as Nozick observes, 'tacit consent isn't worth the paper it's not written on'.[85] There are a number of reasons why a transfer may fail to be voluntary: as Nozick indicates, 'some people steal from others, or defraud them, or enslave them, seizing their product and preventing them from living as they choose, or forcibly exclude others from competing in exchanges', and 'none of these are permissible modes of transition from one situation to another'.[86]

Theft, fraud, enslavement, and so forth are self-explanatory. What are less self-evident are two possibilities that Nozick does not mention. These are duress (other than through any of the actions Nozick alludes to) and mistake (as opposed to fraud). Even if all of these possible reasons are absent and an exchange is genuinely voluntary there is a further requirement for it to be just: this is that it satisfy a Lockean proviso.

Duress

If you (credibly) threaten to shoot me unless I give you my property, or work for you, then, if I accede, I do so only under duress, and thus without consenting. But if I must either work for you or starve, though not through any action of yours, do I consent? If workers must work for capitalists at whatever wage is offered or starve do they do so voluntarily? More generally, do I act voluntarily if the (best) alternative to my undertaking some specific exchange is particularly unattractive?

Cohen claims that I do not, for 'when I am forced to do something I have no *reasonable* or *acceptable* alternative course', but it need not be the case that 'I have no alternative whatsoever'.[87] Cohen's interpretation of what is meant by being forced is not convincing. Any choice I make is necessarily a choice between alternatives: if I have only one option then I am not making a choice. If I have two options, X and Y (defined in such a way as to be mutually exclusive) and I choose X then I reveal my preference for X, which is to say that I find Y relatively unattractive. My choice of X is not by that fact forced: if it were then the notion of unforced choice would be empty, for all choice would be forced. To invoke, as Cohen does, the concept of 'reasonable or acceptable alternatives' is to introduce some arbitrary conception of the good: reasonable or acceptable to whom? The same argument applies however many options I may have, and however relatively unattractive I find Y. Indeed, the concept of my finding Y *much* less attractive than X necessarily involves some cardinal measurement of utility. As was noted in Chapter 1, such measurement is without meaning. (Aristotle goes further, and claims that actions done because of fear of greater evils, even 'when a tyrant tells you to do something shameful, when he has control over your parents and children, and if you do it, they will live, but if not, they will die', are voluntary because 'at the time they are done they are choiceworthy, and the goal of an action accords with the specific occasion; hence we should also call the action voluntary or involuntary on the occasion when he does it'.[88])

The difference between your threatening to shoot me unless I work for you and my starving if I do not work for you is that in the former case the alternative to my working for you would be the result of your acting illegitimately (by violating my rights of self-ownership, if the threat were executed) while in the latter it would be the result of the world being the way it is (and not of any action of yours). What would make my choice non-voluntary would not be that the alternative was *unappealing*, but that it was *illegitimate*. As Nozick expresses it,

> Whether a person's actions are voluntary depends on what it is that limits his alternatives. If facts of nature do so, the actions are voluntary. (I may voluntarily walk to someplace I would prefer to fly to unaided.) Other people's actions place limits on one's available opportunities. Whether this makes one's resulting action non-voluntary depends upon whether these others had the right to act as they did.[89]

Cohen claims that Nozick's interpretation of voluntary 'has the absurd upshot that if a criminal's imprisonment is morally justified, he is then not forced to be in prison'.[90] This, however, is questionable. Nozick's final sentence in the above quotation is unfortunately vague. Cohen interprets it as saying that 'if you *have not* acted in an illegitimate way then my action *is not* forced'. But this cannot be correct, for it would imply that if you encourage me (which is not illegitimate) to fly unaided rather than walk then I am not forced to walk. The correct interpretation of Nozick's statement must be 'if you *have* acted in an illegitimate way (and this prevents my taking an action that I would otherwise have chosen) then my action *is* forced'. This says nothing one way or the other about the imprisoned criminal's possible actions. Wolff makes a claim that is similar to Cohen's in stating that Nozick's interpretation implies that 'miners, trapped underground by a rockfall, are not forced to remain where they are until they are rescued'.[91] The correct interpretation of Nozick's position says nothing one way or the other about the miners' possible actions, any more than it says, or could say, anything about any other (supposed) physical impossibility.

Nozick illustrates his position with another mating example. Simplifying this somewhat, assume that there are three males and three females all of whom want to mate monogamously (and, though Nozick, writing in 1974, does not specify this, heterosexually). Also assume that there is an agreed ranking in terms of 'desirability as … partners': the males are ranked A, B, C, and the females X, Y, Z, each in decreasing order of preference. Then A and X voluntarily choose to mate, each preferring the other to anyone else. Now B would prefer to mate with X, and Y would prefer to mate with A, but as neither of these matings is possible B and Y mate. However, 'their choices are not made nonvoluntary merely by the fact that there is something else they each would rather do', for 'this other most preferred option requires the cooperation of others who have chosen, as is their right, not to cooperate'. This leaves C and Z with the choice of mating with each other or with no one. Again, 'the fact that their only other alternative is (in their view) much worse, and the fact that others chose to exercise their rights in certain ways, thereby shaping the external environment of options'[92] does not mean that they do not choose voluntarily.

A parenthetical point to note in connection with the example of my working for you is that, although Nozick considers it as such, it is not obvious that this is an example of transfer. Nozick sees my working for you as my transferring my labour to you, but it is not clear that I can in fact transfer my labour. The argument that I own my labour relies on the claim that I own myself and my labour is an inseparable part of me. But although I have many ownership rights in myself it has been argued that I cannot alienate myself by selling myself into slavery. Locke claims that 'a man, not having the power of his own life, *cannot*, by compact, or his own consent, *enslave himself* to any one';[93] and Grunebaum argues that the 'permanent alienation of one's self or labor to others is not included in the rights of title [to oneself] because such a right is incompatible with autonomy'.[94] If I cannot permanently alienate my labour it is not clear that I can alienate it by the hour. (A formulation of a principle that is similar to that of justice in transfer but avoids this problem is proposed in Chapter 5.)

Mistake

A mistake in connection with a transaction may concern the effect of the transaction or the nature of the transaction. If I exchange my apple for your orange because I believe that I will enjoy the orange but discover at the first bite that I detest it then I am mistaken about the effect of the transaction. However, it may be that I am not getting an orange at all but a tangerine, either because I did not make sufficient enquiries or because you misled me. If I failed to make sufficient enquiries then I am mistaken about the nature of the transaction; if you misled me then there has been fraud. The distinction between mistake and fraud mirrors that between limits on choice imposed by nature and those imposed by other people who had no 'right to act as they did'. Mistake is a facet of nature; fraud one of other people acting illegitimately.

Mistake, in either of its forms, does not make an exchange non-voluntary. My making a mistake may be interpreted either (a) as my making an error, in that if I were to reconsider my decision more carefully I would change it, or (b) as what I had expected, after careful consideration, not in fact materializing. The first of these must be my responsibility: if I am an autonomous being then I must be responsible for my actions. The second is inescapable: the world is uncertain and what I believe to be the case will not always be the case. If a mistake of this type were to make a transaction non-voluntary there would be no way of determining whether or not any transaction were voluntary. Beliefs are subjective: if I buy an orange-coloured fruit that, after due inspection and enquiry, I believe has a 99 per cent chance of being an orange, and it turns out to be a tangerine, this says nothing about the voluntary or non-voluntary nature of my choice. The position is the same if I buy an orange that I believe with 90 per cent probability that I will enjoy but do not. Wolff claims that 'a number of Nozick's critics … have exposed a chink in Nozick's armour', asking the question 'if a mistake about the nature of a transaction can render it non-voluntary, what about a mistake about its consequences?'.[95] There would appear to be no chink in Nozick's armour here: neither mistake renders the transaction non-voluntary.

A proviso

Justice in transfer also involves the satisfaction of a Lockean proviso. This is both indirect and direct. It is indirect in that I cannot legitimately transfer to you something that has been acquired, by me or by anyone else, in violation of the proviso for that thing is not rightfully mine to transfer. But the proviso is also direct, in that I may not by a series of transfers, each of which is legitimate on its own, acquire property that does not leave enough, and as good, for others. As Nozick expresses it,

> Each owner's title to his holding includes the historical shadow of the Lockean proviso on appropriation. This excludes his transferring it into an agglomeration that does violate the Lockean proviso and excludes his using it in a way, in coordination with others or independently of them, so as to violate the proviso by making the situation of others worse than their baseline situation.[96]

The Lockean proviso would prevent my acquiring all the drinkable water in the world, for that would clearly not leave enough for others. It might also appear to prevent my purchasing all the drinkable water and charging what I will for it, for that would have the same effect: it is an action that would make others worse off. This, however, is more problematic, for the vendors voluntarily sold their supply to me, and should have known the consequences of doing so; and others had the opportunity to purchase some of the supply, with the same knowledge, but chose not to avail themselves of this opportunity.

The proviso would also prevent my acquiring the only water hole in a desert and charging what I will for it. What is less clear is whether the owner of the water hole may charge what he will if there are many water holes in the desert and all of them except his become dry. Nozick claims that he may not: 'this unfortunate circumstance, admittedly no fault of his, brings into operation the Lockean proviso and limits his property rights'. The argument for this conclusion is not transparent, particularly as 'the situation would be different if his water hole didn't dry up, due to special precautions he took to prevent this'. Nozick emphasizes that it is not that owners have rights but these may be overridden to avoid some catastrophe, but rather that it is considerations internal to the theory of property itself that bring the proviso into play, though it is not clear what these considerations are. (Transparency is not improved by Nozick's observation that 'the results, however, may be coextensive with some condition about catastrophe'.[97])

The Lockean proviso does not come into effect simply because the owner of the sole water hole controls the supply of something necessary for others to stay alive: it comes into effect because some appropriation has made people worse off. Nozick contrasts this case with the case of a medical researcher who synthesizes a new drug that treats some disease and only sells this on his own terms (or withholds it). This does not worsen the situation of others for the materials that he uses are readily available, and his using them did not violate the Lockean proviso. His actions no more violate the proviso than do those of the only surgeon able to perform some operation who eats readily available food in order to be able to work. Accordingly, and in contrast with the water case, someone may buy, and then sell on his own terms (or withhold), the total supply of the synthesized drug without violating the proviso. Nozick uses this example to emphasize the fact that the Lockean proviso is not an end-state principle: it is concerned with *the way* in which actions affect others, not with *the result* of these actions.

Justice in rectification

Nozick's basic schema applies to a world that is 'wholly just'. However, the world may not be wholly just: people may have violated the principle of justice in acquisition, for example, by appropriating so much of a thing that insufficient is left for others; or they may have violated the principle of justice in transfer, for example, by theft or fraud. Then, as Nozick observes, 'the existence of past injustice (previous violations of the first two principles of justice in holdings) raises the third major topic under justice in holdings: the rectification of injustice in holdings'. Nozick identifies a number of questions that this raises: if past injustice has shaped present holdings in ways that are not identifiable, what should be done; how should violators compensate the victims; how does the position change if compensation is delayed; how, if at all, does the position change if the violators or the victims are no longer living; is an injustice done to someone whose holding which was itself based upon an injustice is appropriated; do acts of injustice lose their force over time; and what may the victims of injustice themselves do to rectify matters? However, these questions are not answered: as Nozick admits, 'I do not know of a thorough or theoretically sophisticated treatment of such issues'.[98]

It is constructive to distinguish between identifiable specific violations of the principle of justice in acquisition or in transfer, that is violations where the violator and the victim exist and are known, and unidentifiable violations. The former cause no problem in principle: justice in rectification obliges the violators to reverse the violation, or, if this is not feasible (for example, if I have eaten my stolen apple) then to compensate the victim appropriately. Unidentifiable violations, however, cause fundamental problems. Nozick suggests that for these some 'rough rules of thumb' will be required 'to approximate the general results of applying the principle of rectification of injustice';[99] however, it is not clear what lies behind these rules of thumb. Some methods of addressing this problem are proposed in Chapter 5.

Conclusions

The strength of Nozick's entitlements theory of justice is that it uncompromisingly respects individual liberty, and thus avoids all the problems associated with patterned approaches to justice. However, by avoiding patterns it introduces its own problems, for in asking how distributions came about, rather than in simply assessing them as they are, Nozick necessarily delves into the mists of time. Here lie the two most significant, and related, problems with Nozick's theory: that of the relatively unsatisfactory nature of the principle of justice in initial acquisition, and that of the predominantly unexplained means of rectifying any injustice resulting from that.

Nozick's theory cannot properly be criticised for not being concerned with equality (of outcome), for it is explicitly libertarian. However, its implications for equality are extreme: it would consider a state of affairs in which some lived in the lap of luxury while others starved as being just, provided that it came about by just means. As George Orwell observed in *Homage to Catalonia*, 'a fat man eating quails while children are begging for bread is a disgusting sight'[100] (even if in *Wigan Pier* he felt that 'one sometimes gets the impression that the mere words "socialism" and "communism" draw towards them with magnetic force every fruit-juice drinker, nudist, sandal-wearer, sex-maniac, Quaker, "nature cure" quack, pacifist, and feminist in England'[101]). Lest Nozick's position seem harsh it should be noted that his theory is orthogonal to compassion, and there is no reason whatsoever why a just state of affairs may not involve the fortunate aiding the starving on compassionate, or any other, grounds: it is simply that this is not *required* by justice. 'Isn't justice to be tempered with compassion?', Nozick asks. 'Not by the guns of the state' is his answer, but 'when private persons choose to transfer resources to help others, this fits within the entitlement conception of justice'.[102]

Since the entitlements theory, essentially, interprets justice as laissez-faire, no mechanism, other than the protection of property rights (and corrections for any improper acquisitions or transfers), is required to achieve it. As indicated in Chapter 1, the entitlements theory maintains both full self-ownership and full resource-ownership.

Notes

1 All references in this chapter that do not specify an author are to Nozick (1974).
2 Page 151.
3 Page 150.
4 Hayek (1976), page 70.
5 Page 151.
6 Davis (1976), section 1.
7 Page 152.
8 Page 153.
9 Page 155.
10 Page 155.
11 Page 156.
12 Pages 156–57.
13 Pages 157–58.
14 Page 160.
15 Hume (1751/1998), 3.2, page 91.
16 Page 163.
17 Hume (1751/1998), 3.2, page 91.
18 Page 164.
19 Page 164n.
20 Page 161.
21 Sen (1970b), page 19 as reprinted.
22 Page 166.
23 Pages 161–162n.
24 Cohen (1995), pages 26–27.
25 Hardin (1968).
26 Pages 169–169n.
27 Page 169.
28 Page 170.
29 O'Neill (1976), page 471.
30 Fried (2011), page 232.
31 Ryan (1977), pages 130–31.
32 Page 161.
33 Nagel (1975), page 147.
34 Ryan (1977), page 133.
35 Vallentyne (2011), page 152.
36 Vallentyne (1998), page 611.
37 Page 172.
38 Cohen (1995), page 67.
39 Pages 30–33.
40 Page 171.
41 Locke (1689/1988), 2.2.6, page 270.
42 Locke (1689/1988), 2.5.27, pages 287–88.

43 Walras (1896/1990), 2.2.3.4, pages 177, 178, 185–86, author's translation.
44 Cohen (1995), page 12.
45 Cohen (1995), page 68.
46 Cohen (1995), page 69.
47 Wolff (1991), pages 7–8.
48 Cohen (1995), pages 243–44.
49 Taylor (2004), section 5.
50 Arneson (1991), page 54.
51 Page 171.
52 Otsuka (1998), page 67.
53 Sandel (2009), chapter 1.
54 Pages 32–33.
55 Rothbard (1973), pages 26–27.
56 Rothbard (1973), page 28.
57 Arneson (1991), page 36.
58 Narveson (2001), page 66.
59 Locke (1689/1988), 2.5.27, page 288.
60 Pages 174–75.
61 Kirzner (1978), page 201 as reprinted.
62 Sterne (1761/1980), 3.34, page 161.
63 Sterne (1761/1980), 3.34, pages 161–62.
64 Gibbard (1976), page 83.
65 Gibbard (1976), section 2.
66 Page 175.
67 Cohen (1995), page 76.
68 Page 176.
69 Gibbard (1976), section 3.
70 Page 178.
71 Steiner (1994), chapter 7.
72 Steiner (2011), section 2.
73 Otsuka (1998), page 81.
74 Otsuka (1998), page 81.
75 Page 175.
76 Otsuka (1998), section 3.
77 Bentham (1843), page 503.
78 Steiner (2012), page 415.
79 Cohen (1995), chapter 3, section 3.
80 Cohen (1995), page 87.
81 Steiner (1978), page 110.
82 Page 181.
83 Kuflik (1982), page 75.
84 Page 181.
85 Page 287.
86 Page 152.
87 Cohen (1983), page 4.
88 Aristotle (ND/1999), 1110a, page 30.
89 Page 262.
90 Cohen (1983), page 4.
91 Wolff (1991), page 85.
92 Page 263.
93 Locke (1689/1988), 2.4.23, page 284.
94 Grunebaum (1987), page 171.
95 Wolff (1991), page 86.
96 Page 180.

97 Pages 180–81.
98 Page 152.
99 Page 231.
100 Orwell (1938), page 154.
101 Orwell (1937), page 206.
102 Page 348, note 48.

5

COMMON OWNERSHIP

In the framework in which justice is interpreted as laissez-faire with compensation for morally arbitrary factors, common ownership theories in the Steiner-Vallentyne vein treat individuals' holdings of external resources as arbitrary, but (at least directly) make no adjustments for their preferences or abilities. Such theories are diverse, but they all have in common the basic premise that individuals are full owners of themselves but external resources are owned by society in common. The theories differ in what they consider to be external resources, and in what is entailed by ownership in common.

A framework

'Common ownership' is not a particularly satisfactory name for the collection of theories to which it alludes. It should not be taken to imply that all such theories require all external resources to be owned by everyone, either in common or jointly. However, other names fare no better. 'Steiner-Vallentyne libertarianism', another proposed option, would imply, incorrectly, that Steiner and Vallentyne were the only contributors. 'Left-libertarianism', yet another proposed option, would, again incorrectly, imply that such theories were on the left of the political spectrum. But, for example, such theories oppose the means testing of benefits, which is conventionally regarded as being a leftist position; and Cohen, from a Marxist, and thus what is conventionally seen as an unambiguously left-wing perspective, considers the concept of self-ownership, which he regards as being at the centre of such theories, to be an 'attractive thought'.[1]

As was noted in Chapter 1, the discussion of common ownership theories follows that of entitlement theories despite the former preceding the latter in the hierarchy of theories based on the factors that each considers to be arbitrary. The reason for this is that modern common ownership theories (despite their nineteenth-century precursors) may be seen as a reaction to and development of Nozick's entitlement theory. In particular, such theories may be interpreted as attempts to remedy the two main deficiencies in Nozick's theory that were identified at the end of Chapter 4, that is, the unsatisfactory treatment of initial acquisition and the unexplained means of rectifying any injustice resulting from it.

Common ownership theories, as entitlement theories, emphasize institutions, or processes, rather than outcomes. In essence, they consider an institution to be just if, firstly, it recognizes self-ownership (as discussed in Chapter 4) and a further principle of liberty which may be called free association (to be discussed below), and secondly, it involves some scheme of intervention on the holding or transmission of external resources that results, if not in common ownership itself, in a distribution of resources that shares some of the aspects of common ownership.

As noted, common ownership theories may be seen as attempts to remedy past injustices. If individual violators and victims can be identified then past injustices cause no great problem: Nozick's principle of rectification of injustice would give a person whose rights have been violated a moral right to receive compensation from the violator. The problem arises where, because of the passage of time, individual violators (or their heirs) do not exist (or are not traceable). In such cases any rights to compensation will have to be (a) due *from* the holders of any property that may reasonably be considered to have been derived from violations and (b) due *to* all members of society communally (or possibly those of a class which could reasonably be considered to have suffered) rather than to identifiable individuals. In the absence of any relevant information such compensation will typically be to all members of society equally.

Common ownership theories may be seen as specifying the 'rough rules of thumb' in Nozick's suggestion that it may be best to see some egalitarian principles of distributive justice 'as rough rules of thumb meant to approximate the general results of applying the principle of rectification of injustice'[2] in the case where much historical information is missing. They may also be seen as accommodating Nozick's recognition that 'the libertarian position I once propounded now seems to me seriously inadequate, in part because it did not fully knit the humane considerations and joint cooperative activities it left room for more closely into its fabric'.[3]

Schemes of intervention should ideally be consistent with the self-ownership and free association principles. However, they may be less than ideal in this respect. As the principle of self-ownership is more fundamental to liberalism than that of free association, violations of the former will constitute more of a cause for concern than those of the latter.

Such schemes should also be judged by the extent to which they avoid unwarranted arbitrariness in treatment. The justification for this requirement is, in essence, the liberal position that 'equals should be treated equally', together with the claim that 'equal' in this context means equal other than in nominal respects: if you and I are identical other than in that we have different names then we are 'equal'; if we also own property that is identical other than in some nominal respects then we are 'equal'; and so forth. The question of what respects are 'nominal' necessarily varies according to the context.

There are four aspects of this requirement. First, two arrangements that are identical in substance but differ in form should be treated identically. For example, my agreeing to work for you in return for my keep should be treated in the same way as my agreeing to work for you in return for a wage of the same value as my keep and (by the same contract) agreeing to buy my keep from you. Second, and by extension, two arrangements that are similar (in some appropriate metric) should be treated similarly. For example, if land is taxed then my holding land outright should be taxed in a similar way to my holding the land under a very long lease at a nominal rent. (This may be made more precise in a limiting sense: for any specified difference in tax, X, however small, there should be some length of lease such that the difference in tax between my holding the land under that lease and my holding it outright is less than X.) Third, if a person is permitted to perform an action A and he is also permitted to perform an action B then he should be permitted to perform the actions A and B (subject to a Lockean proviso, as discussed in Chapter 4, if applicable). For example, if you are permitted to bequeath property to your nephew and are also permitted to bequeath property to your niece then you should be permitted to bequeath property to your nephew and your niece. Fourth, arrangements, and in particular tax systems, should be time-independent, in that the total tax payable in a week, say, should be the same whether the tax is levied daily or weekly.

Self-ownership

The principle of self-ownership is discussed in Chapter 4: the only aspect of this that requires further development is the way in which it may be disaggregated into its component parts.

In legal terminology, full ownership involves the satisfaction of various incidents of ownership. Of the eleven (to some extent overlapping) standard incidents of ownership set out by Honoré those which most directly apply to the ownership of oneself are the right to possess ('to have exclusive physical control'[4]), the right to manage ('to decide how and by whom the thing owned shall be used'[5]), and the right to the income (that is, both the right to enjoy the thing personally and the right to receive monetary reward from the thing).

However, I may have some but less than full ownership, that is, my ownership may satisfy some but not all of the standard incidents. (This is implicit in Nozick's acceptance that 'one person can possess one right about a thing, another person another right about the same thing'.[6]) It is constructive to distinguish between two classes of rights that I may have over my body: (a) the rights not to have my body violated, for example, by the removal of an eye as in Wolff's eye lottery, and to apply my body as I see fit, for example, by playing basketball, as did Nozick's Wilt Chamberlain; and (b) the right to the fruits of applying my body, for example, to the money that others may be prepared to pay to watch me play basketball.

Loosely, the rights of the first class, or control rights, correspond to the incidents of possession, management, and the non-monetary part of the incident of income; and those of the second class, or income rights, to the monetary part of the incident of income. Note that, notwithstanding the slave analogy (which is in any event limiting, as slavery is something that is absolute), I can lack full self-ownership without being a 'partial slave'. I may have a duty to help you, and thus not be a full self-owner, without your having the right to receive that help, or having any ownership of me.

If I have control rights over myself then I will enjoy 'full and exclusive rights of control and use' over myself. I will also owe 'no service or product to anyone else' in the sense that I am not obliged to create any service or product. However, control rights alone do not imply that if I do create some service or product and sell it then I am entitled to retain the proceeds of sale: that also requires income rights.

Free association

The motivation for introducing a principle of free association is that what is legit-imate for you and for me should be legitimate for us, subject to the satisfaction of the Lockean proviso if this is relevant. This principle is expressed in terms of property, which comprises both property in oneself and in external goods, rather than, as in Nozick's schema, holdings, which, although not defined, by implication comprise external goods only.

A principle of free association that embodies this motivation is that each person has a moral right to combine any property to which he is entitled with the (entitled) property of other consenting persons (and share in the benefits from such combination in any manner to which each person agrees) provided that this does not affect any third parties.

There are three aspects of this principle that require discussion: its foundations, its connection with Nozick's principle of justice in transfer, and its connection with the principle of self-ownership.

Foundations

The basic justification for the principle of free association is that if you and I each own our individual selves and our individual property it would seem arbitrary for us not to jointly own our joint selves and joint property, if we so chose, and if no one else were affected. As Nozick observes, a liberal state 'allows us, indivi-dually or *with whom we choose*, to choose our life and to realize our ends and our conception of ourselves, insofar as we can, *aided by the voluntary cooperation of other individuals*'.[7]

Liberalism, which Cohen interprets as 'the thesis that each person has full private property in himself (and, consequently, no private property in anyone else)',[8] requires that each person may do in private anything that does not impinge on anyone else: he may eat his food raw, or cook it. In its more general sense, liberalism also requires that two people may do in private anything that does not impinge on anyone else: they may eat their own food raw, share their food with one another, cook their own food individually, or cook their joint food together. Arneson makes a similar argument:

> Consider this familiar principle: *people* should be left free to do whatever *they* choose unless their actions cause (or threaten to cause) harm, in specified ways, to non-consenting others. The principle is foundational for one tradition of political liberalism, that inspired by the writings of John Locke, and recently refurbished and defended by Robert Nozick.[9]

A further reason for requiring the principle of free association is that any interventions that violate this principle will also violate the Pareto criterion. If some intervention prohibits you and me from combining our properties in some manner that we would each have chosen, and which does not affect any third parties, then it makes each of us worse off, for we would not have chosen this combination if it would not have benefited each of us; and the prohibition makes no one better off because our combination would not have affected anyone else. Thus the intervention is a Pareto deterioration. (This is not to say that the free association principle *ensures* a Pareto efficient outcome: Prisoners' Dilemmas, public goods, externalities, and so forth provide well-known counter-examples.)

And justice in transfer

The principle of free association is similar in spirit to the principle of justice in transfer set out in Clause 2 of Nozick's schema, which specifies that each person has a moral right to transfer a holding to which he is entitled to another person, provided that each party consents to the transfer and that the transfer does not violate the Lockean proviso.

It is clear that the principle of free association implies that of transfer. If you and I can combine our property as is permitted by the principle of free association then I can certainly transfer my holding to you with your consent. However, the principle of transfer does not imply that of free association, for at least two reasons.

One reason concerns gifts. The principle of transfer states that I have the right to give my property to you, but it does not (at least explicitly) state that you have a right to receive that property free of any encumbrance. For example, Vallentyne claims that 'the right to transfer property to others does not guarantee that others have the power to acquire those rights by means of transfer'.[10] This claim is considered later.

A more significant reason concerns joint enterprise, that is, an activity undertaken by a number of people none of whom alone produces any identifiable part of the outcome. For example, if you sow some grain and I reap it then no identifiable part of the harvest can be attributed to you, or to me: without you there would be no harvest, and without me there would be no harvest. Suppose, then, that you are a skilled sower and I a skilled reaper. The principle of free association says that we have the right to cultivate our lands by your sowing and my reaping, and to divide the produce between us in any manner we see fit. This is achieved by your putting your sowing-labour into the pot, my putting my reaping-labour into the pot, and our each taking from the pot, in some agreed fashion, the grain that is the benefit of our cooperation. The principle of transfer does not imply that right. It might allow you to sell your labour to me, or me to sell mine to you, but that is not the same. It might be argued that an equivalent result could be achieved under the principle of transfer by introducing as a third party a firm, of which you and I were the members, and then specifying various exchanges between each natural person and the firm. However, this requires the introduction of non-natural persons, which would seem alien in the context of distributive justice.

Nozick seeks to avoid the problem of joint enterprise by reducing it to a series of exchanges: 'let us now drop our assumption that people work independently, cooperating only in sequence via voluntary exchanges, and instead consider people who work together jointly to produce something ... once again we have a situation of a large number of bilateral exchanges'.[11] However, this is somewhat misleading. Individuals are not involved in *bilateral exchanges*, for they are not exchanging their labour, or anything else: rather, they are entering into *agreements* (and often *multilateral* ones), at least in those cases, such as that of the sower and the reaper, where no identifiable part of the product can be attributed to either party. The sower cannot be construed as exchanging his labour with the reaper in return for some identifiable part of the harvest in the future for the reaper has (in the absence of an agreement) no rights to any such part of the harvest.

The principle of free association thus avoids a potential problem with the principle of justice in transfer discussed in Chapter 4: that it is not clear that I can in fact sell my labour to you, as opposed to working with you.

And self-ownership

As well as being similar in spirit to the principle of justice in transfer the principle of free association also shares something of the spirit of the principle of self-ownership: it says that a family, say, owns itself in the way that an individual owns himself. Arneson characterizes self-ownership as 'the moral principle that *one* ought to be left free to do whatever *one* chooses so long as non-consenting other persons are not thereby harmed';[12] analogously, the principal of free association may be characterized as 'the moral principle that *people* ought to be left free to do whatever *they* choose so long as non-consenting other persons are not thereby harmed'. The notion of a group of people 'owning itself' is used, in this analogy, with no metaphysical overtones. It means only that the group is self-determining, in that, if no-one outside the group is affected, it may choose to act as it sees fit; and it may make its collective choice according to any constitutional process which it may have adopted. Although the two principles are similar in spirit, the principle of free association does not imply that of self-ownership: the former is explicitly expressed in terms of 'other persons' whereas the latter concerns only the self. And neither does the principle of self-ownership imply that of free association. Self-ownership would permit me to perform a personal service for you, that is, give my labour to you, but it would not (directly) permit me to give my external property to you.

The difference between the two principles is demonstrated by the fact that the Lockean proviso applies to free association but not to self-ownership, as the discussion of drinkable water and a synthetic drug in Chapter 4 illustrates. Nozick notes that 'if the proviso excludes someone's appropriating all the drinkable water in the world, it also excludes his purchasing it all'. In contrast, however, 'a medical researcher who synthesizes a new substance that effectively treats a certain disease and who refuses to sell except on his terms does not worsen the situation of others',[13] and thus does not violate the Lockean proviso. The first case, through the 'purchasing' involved, relates to the principle of free association; the second relates to that of self-ownership. As Vallentyne makes clear, 'there is no [Lockean] proviso ... on initial self-ownership'.[14]

Intervention schemes

Schemes of intervention on the holding or transmission of property (both in oneself and in external goods) may take the form of absolute restrictions on what one may do with one's property, including restrictions on the terms on which one may transfer it to others, or of taxes on the holding or transfer of that property. The latter is of the more interest as taxes will typically be Pareto superior to absolute restrictions. If the drinking of milk is prohibited absolutely then no one may drink. If it is taxed, and the proceeds of the tax distributed to everyone in some fashion, then drinkers are better off than they would have been under prohibition: if they were not then they would not have drunk. Non-drinkers are also better off, for they drink the same amount of milk (that is, none) yet receive part of the taxes generated.

A requirement of all schemes that involve the levying of a tax on holdings, and which satisfy the principle of free association, is that the tax be at a constant rate: if it were not then the total tax paid by two or more people would depend on how they had allocated their holdings between themselves, in contravention of that principle. For example, suppose that there is a tax on wealth at the rates of 10 per cent up to $1m and of 20 per cent above that, and that your wealth is $2m and mine nil. Then if we do not reallocate our holdings between us the total tax payable will be $0.3m, but if we share our wealth equally, as the principle of free association would permit, the tax payable will be $0.2m.

A problem that is shared by all schemes which involve the levying of taxes is that of valuing the property that is to be taxed. This does not require the institution of money: values may be expressed in terms of any numéraire commodity. However, for simplicity of exposition it will be convenient to refer to values in monetary terms. In principle, valuation could be avoided if all property were continuously divisible, such as is gold, for then a tax of 10 per cent on my holding of a kilogram of gold could be met by my delivering 100 grams. However, many items of property, such as tractors, are not divisible, and in that case the tax would need to be levied on the value of tractors.

In an ideal Walrasian world, that is, a world in which all markets function perfectly, the market price of gold is its value to everyone who holds it, in the sense that if someone owned a kilogram of gold and valued gold at more than the market price then he would have bought another gram (which, by hypothesis, he did not), and if he valued gold at less than the market price then he would have sold a gram (which, again by hypothesis, he did not). (This ignores the position of someone who owns no gold: he could value gold at less than the market price, but not more.) Note that it is incorrect to claim that someone could value gold at more than the market price but not buy it because he could not afford it: the value that he ascribes to a gram of gold is simply the amount of something else (money, say) that he would be prepared to forego in order to have it. However, the world may not be ideal in the Walrasian sense (because of missing markets, or monopolies, or externalities, for example) in which case a market valuation may not exist, or, if it does, may not be relevant. (As Nozick wisely observes, 'this is hardly the place to trace the serpentine windings of theories of a just price'.[15]) Notwithstanding these difficulties, all schemes that involve redistribution necessarily assume that the relevant property may be satisfactorily valued, though they will differ in what counts as relevant property.

A further problem that is shared by all schemes that involve taxes is that the tax may affect people's behaviour. This is both a moral and a practical problem. It is a moral problem in that changing peoples' behaviour both diminishes their autonomy and compromises impartiality between rival conceptions of the good. It is a practical one in that if peoples' behaviour is changed significantly the tax may generate little revenue to redistribute. Any tax that changes the relative attractiveness of the options available to people will influence their choice among those options: taxes on earnings will affect how much people work (even if they are not, as Nozick claims, 'on a par with forced labor'); taxes on capital will affect how much people save; and taxes on specific goods, such as milk, will affect how much of these goods people consume. Even taxes, such as poll taxes, which do not change the relative attractiveness of various options will affect behaviour: if as a result of a poll tax I am poorer then I must either consume less or work more.

Interventions on the holding or transmission of property may be seen as falling into three classes: interventions on self-ownership, interventions on the transfer of property, and interventions on the holding of property. And, since any proposal that would result in taxes that form a social fund would be incomplete without a parallel discussion of the application of that fund, a fourth matter to be discussed is the distribution of the social fund. The allocation of arguments between these classes is, in some cases, arbitrary. For example, an argument based on the view that I today am not the same person as I was yesterday may be seen as an intervention on transfer (between my two incarnations) or as an intervention on the holding of property (from yesterday to today).

Interventions on self-ownership

Restrictions on self-ownership are best seen in the light of a decomposition of the various aspects of ownership. Christman[16] distinguishes between control rights and income rights. He claims that control rights differ fundamentally from income rights in four (overlapping) ways. First, the justification of control rights must be based on individualist interests such as liberty, autonomy, and self-determination. The justification for income rights, however, must be based on principles that govern the pattern of the distribution of goods in society, considerations that are not reducible to those individualist interests. Second, the value of a person's control rights depends solely on his personal characteristics. The value of his income rights, however, depends on the distribution of wealth in the society at large and on the preferences of the other members of the society. Third, my control rights are unconditional, in that they are guaranteed by a duty on all other persons not to interfere with my possession, management, and rights to alienate and transfer. Income rights, however, are conditional, for no one has a duty to transact with me and supply me with income. Fourth, and in summary, control rights are individual, whereas income rights depend on the institution of the market, which is a social construct.

Because of these differences, and in particular the claim that income rights depend on society while control rights do not, Christman maintains that it is legitimate to levy taxes on income for redistributive purposes:

> The state must sever its protection of control rights from the structuring of income rights which it utilizes to equalize resources. In this scenario, there would be a redistributive tax on all goods produced, the proceeds from which would be used to distribute to those who are comparatively worse off, in effect, to maintain equality. ... The suggestion is that individuals would be allowed to exercise their talents freely, but all the 'profit' from this exercise would be redistributed on a per capita egalitarian basis.[17]

Although this quotation refers to 'all goods *produced*' it is clear that what is meant is 'all goods *that are traded*'. For example, Christman refers to 'the very existence of a market, without which income rights would not exist'. He notes that income rights arise 'when an individual sells a thing that one [sic] owns (for money, say)'. And he repeatedly refers to 'trade' in the context of income rights. On the other hand, control rights clearly include the right to consume one's goods. For example, 'the central idea of these rights is that the owner maintains primary say over what is to be done with the thing insofar as this affects only the owner'; 'the components of ownership that comprise personal control and *consumption* ... must be justified according to importantly different considerations from those that justify the right to gain income'; and control rights permit that 'I enjoy my property privately – I *consume* it, for example – whether or not others around me consume theirs'.[18]

There are three problems with this proposal. The first is that it involves an unwarranted distinction between income and consumption. If we ignore saving (or treat saving as future consumption), income *is* consumption. A standard definition of a person's income, that of Hicks, is 'the maximum value which he can consume during a week and still expect to be as well off at the end of the week as he was at the beginning'.[19] Accordingly, there is an unwarranted distinction between income rights, which involve income, and control rights, which involve consumption. If I grow and consume some wheat on my own land I am exercising my control right, but not my income right. Yet the wheat that I consume *is* my income. Income is income, whether it is traded or not.

The second problem is that the proposal creates an unwarranted arbitrariness. If I consume my own wheat, and you consume your own oats, then neither of us has any income in Christman's sense: neither of us would be taxed. But if I exchange my wheat for your oats, and I consume the oats and you the wheat, then our aggregate consumption is unchanged, yet we both have income: we would both be taxed. If each member of a family cooks his own meal and washes his dishes then no one has income and no one is taxed; but if one member cooks and another washes then each has income (the value of the service rendered) and each is taxed. This is to say that the proposal violates the principle of free association. Under this, if I had a moral right to my wheat and you to your oats then we would jointly have the moral right to exchange our property (provided that, as is assumed here, no one else was affected); and families could organize their kitchen activities as they saw fit.

The final problem is that the underlying justification for the proposal to tax income rights but not control rights is that the former, but not the latter, arise through a social construct, namely the market, and, as the market is a creation of society, society may rightfully claim some of the benefits that it produces. This however, relies on an entity, the market, of dubious ontological status. It may be useful to refer to 'the market' as a shorthand for a myriad of individual exchanges, but the market is nothing more than this: every transaction in the market is simply an exchange between two individuals. Nozick's observations on distribution apply equally to the market: 'in a free society, diverse persons control different resources, and new holdings arise out of the voluntary exchanges and actions of persons'.[20] (By analogy, it is not uncommon to refer to the marriage market, but that too is but a shorthand for individual matings: each marriage involves a contract between two individuals just as each exchange of produce does. As has been noted, Nozick observes that, 'there is no more a distributing or distribution of shares than there is a distributing of mates in a society in which persons choose whom they shall marry'.)

On the other hand, it might be argued that all (traded) income is the product not only of one's own labour but also the product of the actions of others, through their voluntary participation in exchange, their respecting the rights of property, and indeed of the similar actions of those who in turn furnish the income of those who purchase the products of one's labour, and so forth; in short, of society as a whole. Then even full self-ownership would not ensure that one had full income rights. However, the same argument would imply that one did not have full control rights either, for in most cases one's ability to exercise these rights depends on the willing participation of others: Mr Chamberlain can only play in a particular basketball team if the team owner consents.

The proposal as it stands is, then, untenable. One aspect of the arbitrariness of the proposal would be removed if the tax were really to be on all goods produced rather than all goods that are traded, but this creates its own problems. If I buy some uncooked food and eat it raw then I have produced nothing, and suffer no tax; but if I cook my food then I have produced something (I have produced cooked food from raw food, fuel, and my labour) and thus do suffer tax. This modification would violate the most basic aspects of the principle of self-ownership.

Interventions on the transfer of property

It might be thought that my rights to my property are empty if they do not permit me to do what I will with it (provided that this does not affect others), and in particular to give it to you. On the other hand, the passing down of wealth through the generations is one of the less intuitively appealing implications of this right. Sharing one's property with one's children may be seen as a natural demonstration of parental love; yet gross disparities in wealth between a child whose distant forebears were wealthy (even if they had acquired their wealth in perfectly legitimate ways) and an otherwise identical child whose forebears were poor may seem arbitrary from a moral point of view.

There are four main ways of reconciling these two positions: restrictions or taxes on all gifts, on all bequests, on intergenerational bequests, and on re-gifting. All of these ways have the practical advantage that it is only the property that is given or bequeathed that need be valued.

All gifts

The first proposal is based on Vallentyne's claim, discussed above, that the right to transfer property to others does not guarantee that others have an unencumbered right to receive that property, and that, accordingly, the receipt of gifts may legitimately be subject to taxation. In Christman's terminology this would be to say that (the donor) having control rights in the property, and in particular the right to give it to someone, does not imply (the donee) having income rights in the property, and in particular the unencumbered right to enjoy it.

There are a number of conceptual problems with this claim. One is that no basis is advanced for introducing such an asymmetry between the right to give and the right to receive. Vallentyne asserts that any sensible theory 'will allow gift-giving and gift-receiving'; the issue is 'whether such transactions may be legitimately subjected to taxation and other restrictions'.[21] This however, does not remove the problem. The whole force of 'allow' vanishes if the allowing is subject to unspecified restrictions: if I am allowed the right to receive a gift from you subject to paying 100 per cent tax on it that is not much of a right. If a right subject to restrictions is to be meaningful the restrictions must be specified. As Steiner observes, many thinkers treat the power to make bequests on a par with the power to make gifts inter vivos, 'which they *correctly* regard as being an unimpeachable incident of natural property rights'.[22] In brief, the proposal violates the principle of free association.

A further problem is that the taxation of the receipt of gifts would be highly intrusive. Every time I do you a favour it would have to be recorded, and you would be taxed accordingly: the whole basis of friendship would be compromised. This applies particularly to gifts of services, such as my helping a blind man cross a street. Indeed, any restriction on gifts of services constitutes a violation of the principle of self-ownership. Further, a tax on the receipt of a service cannot be extracted as a percentage of the gift: the blind man cannot hand over ten per cent of his street crossing. It would require the recipient to find the tax from another source: to work for longer in the workshop for the blind. (Gifts would have to include those of services for if they did not then arbitrary distinctions would occur. If I make you a table using my labour but your timber then no gift would arise; but if I employ a carpenter to make the table and then give it to you a gift would arise. The two actions differ in form only, not in substance.)

All bequests

The motivation underlying the second proposal is, in Steiner's words, 'that an individual's deserts should be determined by reference to his ancestor's delinquencies is a proposition which doubtless enjoys a degree of biblical authority, but its grounding in any entitlement conception of justice seems less obvious'.[23] Steiner's later argument[24] in support of this position is that, contrary to Nozick's view, bequests are fundamentally different to gifts inter vivos. Put simply, dead people do not exist, so cannot make gifts. In more detail, the basis for this argument is that transfers of ownership involve an exchange of correlatives. If I transfer my land to you I thereby transfer to you, with your consent, the rights that I held against you with respect to that land. My right that you not interfere with my possession of the land is replaced by your right that I not interfere. Correlatively, your duty not to interfere is transferred to me. You are released from your old restriction and I acquire a corresponding restriction. Purported transfers of ownership by bequest do not have this property: I, as a testator, acquire no restriction whatsoever in assigning ownership to you only posthumously. A testator of land, unlike a donor, cannot possibly incur a duty not to interfere with the recipient's possession of the land for the simple reason that the testator does not, at the relevant time, exist: the purported transfer takes place only at the instant of death. Although there may be a legal right of bequest this is founded on a legal fiction. Such fictions have their uses in overcoming technical difficulties in law, but have no moral force: there are no legal fictions in the state of nature. Accordingly, Steiner concludes that:

There can be no *moral* counterpart to the *legal* power of bequest. So the justification of bequest, if there is one, cannot lie in the demands of justice. And the property of the dead thereby joins raw natural resources in the category of unowned things: things to an equal portion of which ... each person has an equal right.[25]

Steiner's suggestion is more compelling than Vallentyne's, but has its own problems. The basic problem is its arbitrariness. It distinguishes radically between deathbed gifts and bequests. Assume that two people, each of whom has made a will leaving his property to his partner, are involved in a car crash. Soon afterwards, both expire, but before doing so one, who has remained conscious, says to his partner 'I give you all my personal property' (which property, it is supposed, can be transferred by an oral declaration); the other injured person, being unconscious, remains silent. One partner receives everything and the other receives nothing.

Further, if I (purport to) bequeath my property to you then on my death that property is deemed to 'join raw natural resources in the category of unowned things'. However, if while I am living I give it to a third party to hold on trust to apply for my benefit, or even as I direct, during my life and then transfer to you there is no problem: at no time has there been no living owner of the property. The two cases differ in form only, not in substance, yet the treatment in each is radically different.

It might be argued that the trust is a legal fiction, but that would be difficult. The basis of the legal fiction argument is that, as Sir William Harcourt (quoted by Steiner) noted in 1894, 'the right of a dead man to dispose of his property is a pure creation of the law, and the state has the right to prescribe the conditions and limitations under which that power shall be exercised'.[26] A trust, however, is not a 'creation of the law', but a private arrangement between living people. If the trust were to be seen as a fiction then under Steiner's proposal you would not be able to give 'to charity': you would be able to give directly to the needy, but not to a charitable trust whose aim was the support of the needy.

Intergenerational bequests

The third proposal is motivated by Nozick's observation that 'bequests that are received sometimes then are passed on for generations to persons unknown to the original earner and donor, producing continuing inequalities of wealth and position' and that 'the resulting inequalities seem unfair'.[27]

To deal with this Nozick proposes that there be a system of inheritance taxes that will subtract from the property a person can bequeath the value of any property that he himself has received in bequests. This would limit the amount that a person could bequeath to the amount he has added to his bequest, that is, everything he has acquired other than through inheritance less everything he has consumed or given away during his life.

In this rule bequests are to be measured in real terms: 'to determine what amount is first to be subtracted in tax, the monetary value of what one had received in inheritance would be calculated in contemporaneous dollars, corrected for inflation or deflation'. And interest is ignored: 'placing an inheritance in a position to earn interest does count, I think, as an earning that may be passed on'.[28]

As Nozick points out, this 'simple subtraction rule does not perfectly disentangle what the next generation has managed itself to contribute – inheriting wealth may make it easier to amass more – but it is a serviceable rule of thumb'.[29] It is, however, subject to the same arbitrariness problem as affects Steiner's proposal: a person may bequeath anything that he has received by way of gifts inter vivos; and he may also give without limit while living. If your ancestors were given valuable property by their living friends or relations and generously passed this on, during their lifetimes, to others, who, after a series of such transfers, gave it to you then your holding of this property would appear to be just as 'unfair' as it would be had it been passed down by a series of bequests, yet it would not be subject to the tax.

Nozick also considers a second rule, that a person may only bequeath property to people who are, at the time of his death, living. However, Nozick rejects this rule on the grounds that if it were legitimate for someone to leave property to his existing grandchildren it would be arbitrary to prevent him from leaving it to his grandchildren who may be born after his death.

Instead, Nozick proposes a more complex rule: 'a person may not bequeath to two unborn persons who are in different generations of descent from some last already existing node of a family tree'. This is in addition to the general rule, that 'subtracted from the estate someone is able to bequeath will be the amount that person has inherited himself'.[30] This rule fails to satisfy the additivity aspect of the non-arbitrariness requirement. It would permit you to bequeath property to your unborn grandchildren, and it would permit you to bequeath property to your unborn great-grandchildren, but it would not permit you to bequeath property to both.

The justification Nozick gives for any restriction on bequests is that property in something comprises a bundle of rights in that thing, such as the rights to use it, exchange it, and bequeath it, and that in bequest not all of these rights are transferred: in particular, the right to bequeath that thing is not transferred, but adheres to the original creator of the thing. However, no argument is given as to why that particular right is not transferred in bequest.

An alternative justification for a restriction on bequests, proposed by Otsuka, is based on a variant of the Lockean proviso that he calls the egalitarian proviso. This is that 'you may acquire previously unowned worldly resources if and only if you leave enough so that everyone else can acquire an equally advantageous share of unowned worldly resources'.[31] Otsuka argues that this proviso must be interpreted as placing some restrictions on bequests, for if the egalitarian proviso were to permit unlimited bequests 'then the members of the first generation could divide all worldly resources among themselves and then bequeath all of their holdings to a very few, leaving the majority of the next generation landless paupers'. Then 'the unlucky many among subsequent generations could complain that the proviso is arbitrarily and indefensibly biased against them'.[32] However, this argument does not relate specifically to bequests. The principle of justice in transfer contains a Lockean-type proviso that operates to exclude the transfer of holdings in a concentrated way, whether this is by purchase, sale, gift, bequest, or otherwise.

Interventions on bequests may be intuitively appealing, but in all their forms they suffer from the arbitrariness problems discussed above. However, unlike interventions on gifts inter vivos they do not violate the principle of free association: this relates only to vivos.

Re-gifting

A fourth scheme, which may be called the re-gifting scheme, accepts that people have rights to make and receive gifts, but not that these rights last for ever. More precisely, the scheme adopts the position that each person has a moral right to make any gifts (inter vivos or by bequest) to any other person (which person has a moral right to receive such gifts), but that any gifts that are deemed to be re-gifted may be subject to taxation. If the gifts a person makes are less than those he receives then the former are deemed to be re-gifted; if the gifts he makes are greater than those he receives then the latter are deemed to be re-gifted. If I have made gifts of $2 and received gifts of $3 then $2 is re-gifted; if I have made gifts of $5 and received gifts of $4 then $4 is re-gifted. More generally, re-gifting is the lesser of (a) gifts made and (b) gifts received. Thus I may freely give to you anything that I have created or earned but not consumed, but if I pass on anything that I myself have been given then this may be taxed.

Operationally, the scheme specifies that periodically each person pays a tax on the lesser of (a) the cumulative value of all gifts he has made during his life and (b) the cumulative value of all gifts he has received during his life, but with an offset of all tax that he has paid previously. Because of the offset, the scheme is time-independent: the total tax someone would pay in any two consecutive periods is the same as the amount he would pay if the two periods were taken together. Gifts made and received are to be measured in real terms, just as in Nozick's subtraction rule; and as in that rule, interest is to be ignored. Gifts made to trustees are taxable in the same way as gifts to beneficial donees. However, trustees are not taxable on any gifts which they in turn make, though such gifts are to be included in the donee's cumulative receipts. This is to avoid double-counting: my giving $1 to a trustee to give to you should be taxed in the same way as my giving you $1 directly.

The main advantage of this scheme is that under it, in Nozick's phrase, 'an inheritance could not cascade down the generations'.[33] If the rate of tax were 100 per cent then inheritance could only persist for one generation; if the rate were less than this then the shadow of inheritance would diminish exponentially. The scheme avoids all the arbitrariness of Steiner's and Nozick's schemes for bequests, though it does retain the informational problems associated with the tax on all gifts.

However, the scheme does violate one aspect of the principle of free association. That principle in its strongest form would say that I have a right to share my property with you irrespective of the source of that property (provided that this source is legitimate). Notwithstanding that, the scheme respects much of that principle: it only excludes our sharing any property that is given *to me*, and the qualifier 'to me' may be construed as meaning given to me for my own use only. This argument is analogous to Nozick's argument on bequests discussed above, that property in something comprises a bundle of rights and that not all of these rights, and in particular the right to re-gift, are transferred in giving. The problem with such arguments is, however, that if the rights attached to gifts, or bequests, or re-gifting, are to considered open to qualification then it is not clear why other rights, such as those of self-ownership and free association, should not also be considered open to qualification. (It might be possible to circumvent this problem by the artificial device of treating all gifts made during the day, say, as being held in escrow until the beginning of the following day, only becoming absolute then. Under this interpretation if I give you some property today then I am deemed to be giving you full title of that property, and you to be assuming full title, only at midnight. Since 'you tomorrow' do not exist today there is no question of 'I today' associating with 'you tomorrow', and thus no violation of the principle of free association. However, this device seems somewhat artificial.)

A somewhat similar scheme was proposed at the beginning of the twentieth century by Rignano.[34] In essence, this taxes first-generation bequests at a low rate, second-generation bequests at an intermediate rate, and third-generation bequests at the rate of 100 per cent. More precisely, the scheme divides a person's estate into three portions: the difference between the value of his estate and the total value of everything he had received during his lifetime by way of gift or bequest (or, this being 1901, dowry); that which he has acquired first-hand from the person who originally accumulated it; and the remainder. The first portion is taxed at some unspecified standard rate, the second at a suggested rate of 50 per cent (which presumably is higher than the standard rate), and the third at 100 per cent. This scheme avoids the problem of deathbed gifts by treating lifetime gifts in the same way as bequests. However, it cannot avoid the problem of property given on trust, and by taxing just three portions it lacks the flexibility of the re-gifting scheme: that scheme would, in effect, and without having to do so explicitly, tax all portions at exponentially decreasing rates rather than in three arbitrary steps.

Interventions on the holding of property

Interventions on the holding of property may be seen as falling into three classes (although the distinction between these is to some extent arbitrary). One seeks to impose taxes on land by virtue of the fact that it is God-given, one on all natural resources by virtue of the fact that they are natural, and one on all property by virtue of the fact that it is property.

Land

The claim that land, by natural right, belongs to all, like the claim that a person belongs to himself, is made by Locke: 'God … hath given the world to men in common'.[35] The claim is developed by a number of the nineteenth-century writers, and is most notably associated with George. It is put most succinctly by Walras in his second theorem and his explication of that:

> *Theorem II* Land is, by natural law, the property of the state.
>
> In other words, land belongs to everyone in common. … Here, the principle of equality applies, which requires that we may all profit equally from the resources that nature provides for the application of our efforts. … The state, being the owner of the land, will be the owner of the profits (Lemma I [The owner of a thing is the owner of the services produced by it]) and of the rents, as well as of the products, consumption, or investments acquired by it with its profits (Lemma II [The owner of a thing is the owner of the price of it]). … Land does not belong to all men of one generation; it belongs to humanity, that is, to all generations of men.[36]

George's argument that land belongs to all is also based on the premise that it was given to all by God: 'the world is the creation of God … he has given to man the material for labor … this material is land'.[37] An alternative argument that does not invoke the deity is that if all individuals are seen as being morally equal then it would be morally arbitrary were one person to be entitled to more than another of some resource which exists independently of anyone's actions. Accordingly, it is only unimproved land, not developed land, which is relevant. In a typical contribution scheme, that proposed by Steiner, each 'owner owes to the global fund a sum equal to the site's rental value, that is, equal to the rental value of the site alone, exclusive of the value of any alterations in it wrought by labour'.[38]

This creates a problem, for it may not be conceptually possible to separate 'the site's rental value' from 'the value of any alterations'. To do this one would need to compute the value added by the alterations. But as Nozick claims, albeit without further argument, 'no workable or coherent value-added property scheme has yet been devised, and any such scheme presumably would fall to objections (similar to those) that fell the theory of Henry George'.[39]

A further problem with this scheme is that it is time-dependent. Assume that I start the year with no land, acquire some in January and dispose of it in December. Then if the tax is levied monthly I will be taxed, but if it is levied annually (at the end of the year) then I will not, despite my having occupied the land for most of the year (although the price at which I dispose of the land may reflect the future tax burden).

Natural resources

Land is not the only natural resource: what other property is to count is not clear. As Steiner notes, in any intervention scheme involving natural resources everything 'turns on the isolation of what counts as "natural"'.[40] There are many candidates. These, as summarized by Fried, include 'gifts and bequests from the preceding generation; all traditional public goods (laws, police force, public works); the community's physical productive capacity; and well-functioning markets'.[41] Wider still is Van Parijs's proposal to include 'the whole set of external means that affect people's capacity to pursue their conceptions of the good life, irrespective of whether they are natural or produced'.[42] And wider yet is Steiner's argument that 'germ-line genetic information is a natural resource',[43] with the implication that people using it to conceive children should be taxed on its value.

The basic problem with this wider class is that, with the exception of gifts and bequests (which have been considered above), it comprises property, such as public goods, which is not in private ownership. An intervention scheme imposes taxes on individuals, often to pay for such things as public goods; it does not tax public goods (and could not, as there is no person on whom to levy the tax) to pay for distributions to individuals.

The annual value of land is its rent, but land is not the only source of rent. Rent, in the sense of economic rent, is the earnings of any factor of production in excess of that required to bring it into use. Land, in the sense of territory, exists without any incentive needed to bring it into use, so its total earnings are rent. If Mr Chamberlain earns, as in Nozick's example, $250,000 in a season but would be content to play basketball for $50,000 then his rent is $200,000. Interpreting natural resources as those factors that generate rent would seem to be a more principled way of widening the class of natural resources than that proposed by Fried.

The factors of production that may generate rent are land, produced capital goods (such as tractors), and labour. Land generates rent because it is, by its nature, limited in supply. A tax on land does not violate the principles of self-ownership or of free association but, as discussed above, it has its own problems. Produced capital goods, as the qualifier 'produced' implies, are not (in the long run) by their nature limited in supply. Thus if they generate rents it is because their supply has been restricted either by individuals combining (as in a monopoly) or by the state ordaining (for example, by granting patents). A tax on the rent from capital goods therefore seems misplaced. If the rent arises through monopoly then it arises because there is a continuing violation of a Lockean-type proviso on free association: the appropriate action would be the prevention of that violation. If it arises from the state granting a patent then it must be presumed that the state intended that the rent would arise (and had already made arrangements to tax it if it saw fit). Labour is naturally limited in supply. It may generate rents by that fact (there is only one Wilt Chamberlain) or, again, by individuals combining (as in a labour union) or by the state ordaining (for example, by restricting entry to a profession). In the first case a tax on Mr Chamberlain's rent, which is a part of the fruits of his labour, clearly violates the self-ownership principle. In the other two cases, labour unions and restricted entry to professions, the observations made in connection with capital goods continue to apply, mutatis mutandis.

A different justification for taxing the 'excess return' on labour is provided by Van Parijs's argument that being in employment may be a form of property:

> Suppose now that we are in a *non-Walrasian economy*, that is, that for some reason the labour market does not tend to clear. This may be because of obstacles to perfect competition, such as minimum wage legislation or union monopolies. ... [Then] the holding of a job constitutes a third type of asset. ... Let us give each member of the society concerned a tradable entitlement to an equal share of those jobs. ... [This] amounts to sharing among all the *employment rents* otherwise monopolized by those in employment. These rents are given by the difference between the income (and other advantages) the employed derive from their job, and the (lower) income they would need to get if the market were to clear.[44]

Again, the observations made in connection with capital goods continue to apply: if the 'employment rents' arise through 'union monopolies' then there is a continuing violation of a Lockean-type proviso on free association that should be addressed directly; if they arise through 'minimum wage legislation' then it must be presumed that the state intended that outcome and had arranged to compensate (if it considered compensation to be due) those adversely affected.

Note that Van Parijs's 'employment rent' is not the same as economic rent. Employment rent is the difference between employees' actual income and 'the income they would need to get if the market were to clear'. Economic rent, however, is the difference between actual income and the income that employees would require to induce them to work. The two will generally differ. Suppose that basketball players less talented than Mr Chamberlain earn $50,000 a season when in a union; that in a competitive market, with no union, they would earn $40,000; and that unionized or not they are prepared to play for $20,000. Then the players' employment rent is $10,000; their economic rent is $30,000.

A final problem with a scheme that taxes all natural resources is that it is time-dependent, for the same reason that a scheme that taxes land alone is.

All property

Taxing property per se, by imposing a periodic tax on it, is similar to taxing bequests: the difference is that the tax is applied periodically rather than at the end of every life. There are three possible justifications for taxing property per se: extending the concept of bequests, removing one of the incidents of ownership, and requiring a fee for protection.

The first justification is based on a deemed lack of personal continuity over time: that 'I tomorrow' am not the same person as 'I today'. If this position is adopted then 'I am holding property overnight' really means 'I today' am bequeathing property to 'I tomorrow'; the property is a bequest not a gift inter vivos as 'I today' cease to exist at midnight. Van Parijs expresses this justification as follows:

> If the person 'I' am now is distinct from the person 'I' shall be tomorrow, whatever the former person leaves to the other must be assimilated to a gift or a bequest. What I save this month is part of the endowment with which the person I shall be next month starts life and must therefore be added to the pool on which it is legitimate to draw.[45]

The second justification involves limiting the rights of ownership in external objects, that is, acknowledging only less than full ownership, specifically by excluding Honoré's incident of the absence of term, that one's rights to property do not expire. As Honoré accepts, 'the listed incidents, though they may together be sufficient, are not individually *necessary* conditions'[46] for ownership. If the incident of the absence of term is excluded then I have no unencumbered right to continue my ownership in some property from today until tomorrow. If I do so, the state may legitimately require that I pay for that privilege.

A third justification employs an alternative to Honoré's classification of the rights to property. This distinguishes between the rights to enjoy and to hold through time. The first does not involve the state in any way, other than in non-interference, but the second may, through the need for protection. As the Bible reminds us, the trouble with laying up treasures on earth is that they are 'where moth and rust doth corrupt, and where thieves break through and steal',[47] and the role of even a minimal state is to protect people's property against theft (even if it has little control over moths and rust). As Nozick observes, 'the most minimal state seriously discussed by the mainstream of political theorists [is] the night-watchman state of classical liberal theory'.[48] If I hold property overnight it is the duty of the night watchman to protect it. If the state is to provide this protection it may legitimately charge a fee for this, and this fee may take the form of a tax on the holding of property.

A specific proposal that these justifications would suggest is that periodically the state levy on the holders of all property a proportionate tax on the value of that property. Under the assumption that all property can be valued this proposal is simply that there be a periodic wealth tax. If the justification for the tax is that of lack of continuity over time or the exclusion of the absence of term then the rate of tax should be the same for all types of property: land used for playing polo is to be taxed at the same rate as land used for playing cricket. This is to ensure that the scheme is neutral with respect to conceptions of the good, such as playing polo being more worthy than playing cricket, or vice versa. (If the justification is protection then the rate may vary according to the type of property, since some types, such as chattels, may be easier to steal than others, such as land.)

The advantages of this scheme in comparison with a scheme involving the taxation of natural resources is that the problem of determining what comprises such resources is avoided. All property is taxed, and at the same rate. Its advantage in comparison with a scheme involving prohibitions of, or taxes on, bequests is that the arbitrariness of transfers on trust and of deathbed gifts is avoided.

There are, however, conceptual problems. One is that although the scheme claims to tax property per se in fact it only taxes external property, that is, all property other than property in oneself: the self-ownership principle dictates that the latter be exempt. This introduces an element of arbitrariness. Suppose that I have spent some of my wealth training to become a brain surgeon and earn fees from practising this profession, and you have spent the same sum on buying a brain scanner that you lease to a hospital. Suppose further that my fee income is the same as your leasing income, and that the life of the brain scanner is the same as my future working life. Then we have the same wealth: mine is in the form of human capital, yours in the form of physical capital. Yet you will be subject to tax but I will not.

A second problem is that the scheme is time-dependent. Assume that I start the week on Sunday with no wealth, each day save a certain sum, and on Saturday spend all my accumulated saving. Then if the tax is levied on a daily basis I will be taxed, but if it is levied weekly (at the end of the week) then I will not.

A final problem is that although the scheme is neutral with respect to conceptions of the good as embodied in different activities today it is not neutral with respect to different conceptions as embodied in the same activity in different time periods. If I spend my income playing polo today but you save yours in order to play polo tomorrow then you will be subject to tax but I will not. More generally, the prudent, who save some of their income, are taxed more than the profligate, who spend all of their income when they receive it, even if the circumstances of each are identical.

A further question concerns property that comprises private wealth but not societal wealth. Land, tractors, and so forth (if in private ownership) comprise the private wealth of their owners, and also the wealth of society: they form the aggregate capital of society. But if I owe you a sum of money this forms part of your wealth (assuming that it is known that I will not default) but not of the wealth of society: your wealth is increased by this sum but my wealth is reduced by the same amount. This distinction suggests two possible variants of the intervention scheme: one in which a person is taxed on his wealth including the (net) value of the claims that he holds on others, and one which excludes such claims. Equivalently, the first variant may be seen as a tax on *persons* based on their holdings of property, and the second as a tax on *property* itself.

Although taxing property rather than persons would seem to fit more naturally in a common ownership framework it may lead to arbitrary outcomes. If I rent you a machine then, it being my property, I am taxed on its value; but if I lend you the money to buy the machine then the machine is your property and I am not taxed on its value, despite the fact that my wealth is the same in each case. Further, taxing property may be considered to be less equitable than taxing persons. If you have lent all your substantial wealth to me to buy land, and I have no other assets, then I would be taxed but you would not, despite your being wealthier than I. (However, in a perfect Walrasian world equilibrating forces will make the differences between taxing property and taxing persons vanish, as is shown in the appendix to this chapter.)

The distribution of the social fund

The common ownership theories discussed above have, typically, involved the imposition of taxes but have not specified how the social fund created by these taxes is to be applied. One natural way to do this is to specify that the social fund be distributed to everyone in equal shares. As has been noted, Steiner sees 'the property of the dead as joining in the category of unowned things *to an equal portion of which each person has an equal right*', and Christman similarly suggests that 'individuals would be allowed to exercise their talents freely, but all the "profit" from this exercise would be redistributed *on a per capita egalitarian basis*'. Each of these mandates equal division. There are, however, other possibilities.

Nozick, with respect to the case where the social fund is collected explicitly to rectify historical injustices, suggests that the fund be distributed in such a way that the end result is close to Rawls's difference principle:

> Lacking much historical information, and assuming (1) that victims of injustice generally do worse than they otherwise would and (2) that those from the least well-off group in the society have the highest probabilities of being the (descendants of) victims of the most serious injustice who are owed compensation by those who benefited from the injustices (assumed to be those better off, though sometimes the perpetrators will be others in the worst-off group), then a *rough* rule of thumb for rectifying injustices might seem to be the following: organize society so as to maximize the position of whatever group ends up least well-off in the society.[49]

An alternative argument leading to a similar conclusion is that while the Lockean proviso on initial acquisition may be satisfied for many through their having benefited from the civilization that the appropriation of unowned resources has brought about, there will be others who have suffered. In Nozick's formulation, 'compensation would be due those persons, if any, for whom the process of civilization was a *net loss*, for whom the benefits of civilization did not counterbalance being deprived of these particular liberties'.[50] However, given Nozick's weak form of the Lockean proviso almost everyone will have benefited, so that under this formulation there will be little, if any, scope for compensation.

Brody adopts a similar line of reasoning, again based on the premise that the worst-off are likely to be those who have suffered most from injustice in initial acquisition. He argues that many will have benefited so much, either directly or indirectly, from previously unowned resources being taken into private ownership that they require no compensation for this, but others may be less fortunate:

> There are, however, the very indigent who do require compensation. Even if they are better off than they would have been if we had remained in the

state of nature, they have not obtained their fair share of the gains which result from the system of property rights developed through Lockean initial acquisitions.[51]

A radically different way of dividing the social fund would be to use it to compensate those with unchosen disadvantages, as would be justified, for example, by the argument that such disadvantages were morally arbitrary. Thus Vallentyne proposes an '*equality-promoting Georgist* conception, according to which the social fund from rents is spent to promote equality of unchosen advantage';[52] this 'focuses spending on the disadvantaged rather than dividing the fund equally'. Similarly, Otsuka claims that 'resources can in principle be divided in a manner that allows a fairly wide range of the disabled ... to better themselves from their holdings of worldly resources to the same degree as the able-bodied',[53] and suggests that they should be. A somewhat different procedure that compensates for unchosen disadvantages is Van Parijs's proposal[54] that the social fund be applied first in compensating for inequalities in personal endowments and then in maximizing the position of those with the least valuable set of opportunities open to them.

There is, however, something perverse about any proposal to apply the social fund in a way that compensates for unchosen personal endowments when all means of collecting the taxes that form that fund have, because of an adherence to the self-ownership principle, clearly ruled out taxing people on that basis. As Fried expresses it,

> The resulting schemes, which judge the tax and transfer sides of fiscal policy by wholly different distributive criteria, seem morally incoherent. If the just state may not take more from the talented by virtue of their unequal talents ... why may it give more to the untalented by virtue of their unequal talents?[55]

A coherent combined tax and distribution scheme would, then, not discriminate in the distribution of the social fund on the basis of attributes that were ruled out in the creation of the fund, that is, in taxation. An advantage of Steiner's proposal to tax 'germ-line genetic information' with its effective redistribution from the parents of the genetically advantaged to those of the genetically disadvantaged is that it passes this coherency test.)

Each of the schemes of intervention discussed above, together with the self-ownership and free association principles, defines an entitlement theory of justice as opposed to a patterned one. As noted in Chapter 4, an entitlement theory specifies that my holdings are just if I am entitled to them by some appropriate principles of justice or, equivalently, under some appropriate process. Under each scheme discussed I am entitled to my holdings according to that scheme: whether or not the scheme is an acceptable principle of justice it is undoubtedly a process, and thus determines an entitlement-based rather than a patterned outcome. It is true that, to take as an example a tax on all property, a pattern, that of equal wealth, would eventually emerge if nothing external to the tax scheme changed, for each year part of the wealth of those with greater wealth would be distributed to those with less. However, as noted in Chapter 4, the process defined by the scheme should be distinguished from any 'strands of pattern' that may run through the set of holdings that results from this process. As has been seen, the fundamental problems with patterns are that under any patterned scheme 'capitalist acts between consenting adults' would have to be forbidden and there would have to be 'continuous interference with people's lives'. The scheme that levies a periodic tax on all property, to continue with this example, necessarily involves periodic interference. But it does not look at any existing pattern, nor explicitly seek to impose any new pattern. An annual property tax of 10 per cent no more forbids 'capitalist acts between consenting adults' or involves a 'continuous interference with people's lives' than does a climate in which 10 per cent of property rusts away (or is corrupted by moths) each year.

A final matter to consider is the size of the social fund, or, equivalently, the specification of the rates of the taxes that generate it. This is a question that cannot be answered a priori. High rates of tax infringe liberties more than low, but foster greater equality of outcome. The only observation that can be made objectively is that higher rates may induce people to avoid the activity or property that is subject to the tax, and thus generate less revenue to redistribute via the social fund.

Conclusions

The strength of common ownership theories is that, as Fried puts it, they 'have staked out a middle ground between the two dominant strains of contemporary political philosophy: the conventional libertarianism of those such as Robert Nozick on the right, and the egalitarianism of those such as Rawls, Dworkin, and Sen on the left'.[56] It is immaterial whether or not such theories are, in Fried's terms, 'just liberal egalitarianism in drag'.[57] If two independent arguments reach the same conclusion each strengthens the appeal of the other.

There are eight interpretations, as defined by their respective intervention schemes, of this middle ground: one involving a limit on self-ownership; four involving interventions of the transfer of property; and three involving interventions on the holding of property. The scheme that limits self-ownership evidently violates the principle of self-ownership. Of those which relate to the transfer of property, the scheme that limits all gifts violates the core of the principle of free association; that which limits all bequests has arbitrariness problems (specifically, as regards deathbed gifts and trusts); that which restricts intergenerational bequests also has arbitrariness problems (in the same way as restrictions on all bequests, and also as regards additivity); and that which taxes re-gifting violates a peripheral aspect of the principle of free association. All schemes that relate to the holding of property suffer from the problem of being time-dependent. The scheme that taxes land alone also suffers from the conceptual problem of determining the value of the site ignoring any alterations to it; that which taxes all natural resources suffers from the conceptual problem of defining such resources; and that which taxes all property has arbitrariness problems (specifically, in that it makes a distinction between physical and human wealth and that it treats the prudent and profligate differently).

In summary, as indicated in Chapter 1, common ownership theories maintain full self-ownership but not full resource-ownership.

Appendix

In a perfect Walrasian world equilibrating forces will make the differences between taxing property and taxing persons vanish.

Assume first that the tax is on property itself. Then if A rents B a machine, it being A's property, A is taxed on its value; but if A lends B the money to buy the machine then the machine is B's property and A is not taxed on its value. However, the net effect will be the same either way, for equilibrating forces will ensure that the rate of interest and the net (that is, after tax) rate of return on real property are the same. Assume that the (annual) rate of tax is t, the market price of the machine (given that) is p, and the machine produces goods to the value of y each year. Then the rental value of the machine is y per year and the net return from owning the machine (as the owner has to pay a tax of tp) is $y - tp$ so that the net rate of return on real property is $y/p - t$, as must be the rate of interest, r. Then if A rents B the machine A will pay tax of tp and receive rent of y; B will pay no tax and pay rent of y (and have goods to the value of y). If A lends B the money to buy the machine A will pay no tax and receive interest of $rp = y - tp$; B will pay tax of tp and pay interest of $rp = y - tp$ (and have goods to the value of y). The effect of the tax is the same either way: A's net income from the activity is $y - tp$ and B's is nil. A tax on property is analogous to a tax on transactions: it makes no difference whether the buyer/renter or seller/owner pays the tax.

Now assume that the tax is on persons. The rental value of the machine is still y per year so that, there being no tax on machines per se, the net rate of return on real property is y/p, as must be the rate of interest. Then whether A rents B the machine or lends B the money to buy the machine A will pay tax of tp and receive rent, or interest, of y. The outcome is the same as under a tax on property itself.

Notes

1 Cohen (1995), page 12.
2 Nozick (1974), page 231.
3 Nozick (1989), pages 286–87.
4 Honoré (1987), page 166.
5 Honoré (1987), page 170.
6 Nozick (1974), page 282.
7 Nozick (1974), pages 333–34, emphasis added.
8 Cohen (1986), page 114.
9 Arneson (1991), page 36, emphasis added.
10 Vallentyne (2000), page 14.
11 Nozick (1974), page 187.

12 Arneson (1991), page 36, emphasis added.
13 Nozick (1974), pages 179–81.
14 Vallentyne (2011), page 163.
15 Nozick (1974), page 186.
16 Christman (1991), section 2.
17 Christman (1991), page 40.
18 Christman (1991), pages 29–34, emphasis added.
19 Hicks (1946), page 172.
20 Nozick (1974), pages 149–50.
21 Vallentyne (2000), page 14.
22 Steiner (1994), page 253, emphasis added.
23 Steiner (1977), page 152.
24 Steiner (1994), chapter 7.
25 Steiner (1994), page 258.
26 Steiner (1994), page 252.
27 Nozick (1989), page 30.
28 Nozick (1989), page 31n.
29 Nozick (1989), page 31.
30 Nozick (1989), page 32.
31 Otsuka (1998), page 79.
32 Otsuka (1998), page 89.
33 Nozick (1989), page 31.
34 Rignano (1901), part 1, chapter 3.
35 Locke (1689/1988), 2.5.26, page 286.
36 Walras (1896/1990), 2.6, page 189, author's translation.
37 George (1897), page 4.
38 Steiner (1994), pages 272–73.
39 Nozick (1974), page 175.
40 Steiner (1994), page 277.
41 Fried (2004), pages 85–86.
42 Van Parijs (1995), page 101.
43 Steiner (1994), page 275.
44 Van Parijs (1995), pages 107–8.
45 Van Parijs (1995), page 102.
46 Honoré (1987), page 161, emphasis added.
47 Matthew 6:19.
48 Nozick (1974), page 25.
49 Nozick (1974), page 231.
50 Nozick (1974), page 179n.
51 Brody (1983), page 83.
52 Vallentyne (1998), page 621.
53 Otsuka (1998), page 86.
54 Van Parijs (1995).
55 Fried (2004), page 90.
56 Fried (2004), page 67.
57 Fried (2004), page 84.

6

AN ASSESSMENT

The preceding chapters have presented a critical appraisal of a number of theories of distributive justice, each of which is interpreted as laissez-faire with compensation for morally arbitrary factors. The present chapter discusses the problems of assessing the relative merits of these theories, and considers the extent, if any, to which they can accommodate both liberty and equality.

Consistency

The question of the degree to which each of the theories discussed is internally consistent has been considered in detail in each of the four preceding chapters.

Dworkin's equality of resources theory may have the greatest problems of internal consistency. As has been noted, some of the problems with Dworkin's auction construction may be avoided by adopting its outcome as a specification of justice in its own right. The insurance scheme, however, has more serious and unavoidable problems. The fundamental flaw is that shown by Roemer's theorem: that no Dworkinian scheme can satisfy four very weak consistency conditions, so that, as Roemer puts it, 'resource egalitarianism is an incoherent notion'.

Rawlsian justice as fairness fares a little better, but, if it is to be grounded in choice from behind a veil of ignorance, has the serious flaws of that construction. Some of these, such as the incoherence of the variable index of primary goods and the impossibility of choosing a feasible distribution when the contractors do not know others' responses, can be avoided by inessential changes. But other problems are unavoidable, particularly those of identifying the least advantaged (with the related problems of defining primary goods and the construction of an index of these), and of the supposedly rational choice of the maximin principle with, as Harsanyi puts it, its 'absurd practical implications'.

Common ownership theories, being diverse, are harder to assess as a group. Theories that limit self-ownership clearly have problems. Those that involve interventions of the transfer of property have a variety of arbitrariness problems, and typically violate some aspect of the principle of free association. Those that involve interventions on the holding of property have, on the whole, some serious arbitrariness problems, particularly as regards the definition of property and time-dependency.

Nozickian entitlements theory may have the fewest problems of consistency. But although they may be few they are not trivial, particularly those relating to justice in initial acquisition, and to the rectification of past injustice.

There is, however, one problem not previously mentioned that affects Nozick's theory alone; and another problem that affects all theories other than Nozick's. The first of these concerns the financing of institutions, such as the rule of law, under which just distributions are to be implemented. If, in Nozick's theory, taxation, being 'on a par with forced labor', is to be avoided then there can be no resources available to finance these institutions, and being entitled to holdings would have little relevance if there were no mechanism to enforce that entitlement. (Protective associations, financed by voluntary contributions, are a separate matter.) None of the other theories discussed face this problem, for they all involve some form of taxation that may be used to implement their prescriptions.

The second problem concerns the assumption made in Chapter 1 that there is some given fixed population. If this assumption is relaxed then a major problem arises for all theories that involve a social fund formed through taxation. The only theory in which it does not arise is Nozick's entitlements theory, which does not involve any social fund. The problem is, what is the relevant population? That is, who are to contribute to and benefit from the social fund? The prescriptions of the various theories will typically depend critically on the answer to this question. To give but one example, Rawls's maximin income distribution if applied nationally, say in Luxembourg, might result in the worst-off Luxembourger having an annual income of the order of $20,000; if applied globally it might result in the worst-off Luxembourger having an annual income of some $500. This question has two aspects: should the relevant class of persons be defined societally or globally; and should it be defined statically or intergenerationally?

There are many reasons why our moral concerns may be local rather than global when they relate to friendship, community, and so forth, but it is hard to find any such reason when our concern is justice. Thus it is difficult to reject the conclusion that justice should involve every person living, wherever they happen to live. As Steiner puts it, 'our moral duties to respect other persons' original rights and the rights derived from them don't suddenly evaporate at international boundaries ... these duties are *global* in scope'.[1]

It may be easier to accept that the social fund should involve only those living today rather than all future generations (if only because future generations will benefit from the physical capital accumulated by earlier generations), but the contrary view is frequently taken. As has been seen, in the context of natural resources

Walras claims that 'land does not belong to all men of one generation; it belongs to humanity, that is, to all generations of men'. More generally, Otsuka proposes 'modifying the egalitarian proviso so that it instead demands acquisitions that leave enough for the members of all generations to better themselves to the same degree'.[2]

Absolute and relative justice

Each of the theories discussed has sought to identify some absolute conception of justice. Since each theory has its own problems it is not clear that it is possible to choose between them, that is, to identify some ideal absolute conception of justice. It might also be argued that, possible or not, this is not constructive.

This is the position adopted by Sen, who identifies a dichotomy in Enlightenment thought: 'there are two basic, and divergent lines of reasoning about justice among leading philosophers associated with the radical thought of the period'. The first approach, associated with Hobbes, Locke, and Kant, is what Sen calls 'transcendental institutionalism'. This concentrates on 'what it identifies as perfect justice, rather than on relative comparisons of justice and injustice'; its focus is on the institutions that characterize this, rather than on the actual societies that these would produce. The second approach, associated with Smith, Marx, and Mill, is what Sen calls 'realization-focussed comparison'. This involves 'comparisons of societies that already existed or could feasibly emerge, rather than ... searches for a perfectly just society'. As Sen observes, 'it is the first tradition – that of transcendental institutionalism – on which today's mainstream political philosophy largely draws in its exploration of the theory of justice'.[3] In Sen's view, the 'most powerful and momentous exposition of this approach can be found in the work of the leading political philosopher of our time, John Rawls'.[4] Sen also identifies Dworkin and Nozick as followers of this approach (and would also, no doubt, include writers in the Steiner-Vallentyne vein among such followers).

Sen claims that 'if a diagnosis of perfectly just social arrangements is incurably problematic, then the entire strategy of transcendental institutionalism is deeply impaired'. He illustrates this problem with his well-known example of three children and a flute. In this (with a change of names) an adjudicator has to decide which of three children should have a flute over which they are quarrelling. Jeremy claims that he should have it because, as he is the only one who can play it, his having it will bring delight to the ears of all. John claims that he should have it because he has no other toys. And Robert claims that he should have it because he has just finished making it, at which point 'these expropriators came along and tried to grab the flute'. All the facts claimed are known to be true. Sen claims that utilitarians (Jeremy), egalitarians (John), and libertarians (Robert) will each 'take the view that there is a straightforward just resolution staring at us here, and there is no difficulty in spotting it'.[5] The problem is, they will differ irreconcilably as to what it is.

Transcendental institutionalism asks 'what would be perfectly just institutions', while realization-focussed comparison asks 'how would justice be advanced'.[6] A little more formally, transcendental institutionalism seeks to identify some absolutely just institution, and realization-focussed comparison seeks to specify an ordering of institutions according to their justness. But importantly, the latter does not seek a complete ordering. The ordering of realization-focussed comparison is thus similar to the Pareto ordering, which also is not complete: two states may each be Pareto efficient without one being superior to the other, or their being equivalent. If realization-focussed comparison did specify a complete ordering then, provided that this were also reflexive and transitive (and if it were not it would be of little value) it would, as noted in Chapter 1, specify some most just institution, at least if there were only a finite number of possible institutions.

As Sen asks, 'would not a theory that identifies a transcendental alternative also, through the same process, tell us what we want to know about comparative justice?'. He suggests that 'we may be tempted by the idea that we can rank alternatives in respect of their closeness to the perfect choice', but identifies two problems with this idea. The first is that 'there are different dimensions in which the objects differ', and there is no obvious way to combine these dimensions. The second is that 'descriptive closeness is not necessarily a guide to valuational proximity': Sen gives the example of someone who prefers red wine to white but prefers either to a mixture of the two even though the mixture is, in 'an obvious descriptive sense'[7] closer to the preferred red. However, these are but two aspects of the same problem: that there is no natural metric on the set of institutions.

It is important to note that transcendental institutionalism seeks to identify an institution that is just in some absolute (and, as the name suggests, transcendental) sense, rather than the 'most just' institution in some given set of possible institutions. If it did the latter then it would determine comparative justice through pairwise comparisons. If the possible institutions are limited to just two and transcendental institutionalism identifies one as the best of these then that one may be considered to be more just than the other; repeating this test for all pairs would give an ordering. (As noted in Chapter 1, choices and orderings are, under rationality axioms, equivalent.)

An impossibility result

As an alternative to Sen's approach the problems of identifying some absolute conception of justice may be seen through a reinterpretation of Arrow's well-known impossibility theorem. Arrow considers a set of states of the world, and a set of individuals each of whom has a preference ordering over these states. Arrow asks how social choices may validly be made, that is, he seeks to specify a rule that combines individuals' preference orderings over the states into a social preference ordering. The social preference ordering is required to be reflexive, complete, and transitive, and also to satisfy four consistency conditions. The first of these is that of universal domain, which requires that all possible patterns of individuals' preference should be admissible. The second is the (weak) Pareto criterion, which requires that if everyone prefers one state to a second then the first should be ranked above the second. The third is independence of irrelevant alternatives, which requires that the social ranking of any two states should depend only on the individuals' rankings of the two. And the fourth is non-dictatorship, which requires that the preferences of no single individual should always dominate.

Arrow shows that there is *no* rule for combining individuals' preference orderings over the states into a social preference ordering that satisfies these four conditions. (A proof is provided by Arrow;[8] simpler versions are also available.[9])

The reinterpretation replaces the set of states of the world with a set of possible conceptions of justice, and the set of individuals with a set of criteria that might be considered desirable in such a conception of justice. The conceptions of justice might be such theories as justice as fairness, equality of resources, entitlements, common ownership, and so forth; and the criteria might be such matters as autonomy, equal respect, and Pareto efficiency. For each criterion there is a ranking of theories, according to how well they satisfy this criterion. For example, if justice as fairness achieved a greater degree of equal respect than entitlements but less autonomy then it would be ranked above entitlements according to the equal respect criterion, and below it according to the autonomy criterion. For ease of interpretation we may consider theories to be given some (ordinal) numerical score for each criterion: justice as fairness would then have a higher score than entitlements on the equal respect criterion, and a lower one on the autonomy criterion.

The problem is to specify a rule that orders the various theories of justice according to how well they satisfy the various criteria. For example, such a rule might say that one theory is more satisfactory than a second if it scores more highly than the second on a majority of the criteria. For such a rule to be of any use the ordering that it specifies would have to be reflexive, complete, and transitive. There are four further requirements that we may reasonably demand of such a rule; these correspond to the four consistency conditions in Arrow's theorem. The first requirement is that the rule be universally applicable, in that it should allow for any possible pattern of scores. The second, an analogy of the Pareto criterion, is that if one theory scores more highly than a second on all criteria then the first should be judged to be more satisfactory than the second. The third is that the rule be independent of irrelevant factors, in that the ranking of two theories should depend only on their respective scores in the various criteria. The fourth is that the rule not be trivial, in that it should not take account of only one criterion.

Then Arrow's theorem, as reinterpreted, says that there is no rule that satisfies these four requirements. There is *no* satisfactory way of assessing theories of justice according to any external criteria.

Liberty and equality

The theories of justice discussed in this book all interpret distributive justice as an expression of laissez-faire with compensations for factors that they consider to be morally arbitrary, and thus for which they make adjustments. They have been organized according to these factors: the Rawlsian theory of Chapter 2 adjusts for preferences, productivity, and external property; the Dworkinian theory of Chapter 3 only for productivity and external property; the Steiner-Vallentyne theories of Chapter 5 only (at least directly) for external property; and the Nozickian theory of Chapter 4 for none of these (other than corrections for any improper acquisitions or transfers). As has been shown, these theories form a hierarchy in terms of the liberties (self-ownership and resource-ownership) that they maintain: the first maintains neither, and does not recognize responsibility; the second maintains neither, but does recognize responsibility; the third maintains self-ownership but not resource-ownership; and the fourth maintains both self-ownership and resource-ownership. And as has also been shown, they form a corresponding hierarchy in terms of equality of outcome: the first is the most egalitarian, followed by the second, then the third, and finally the fourth as the least egalitarian.

The theories thus accommodate liberty and equality in ways which are not immediately commensurate. One possible source of a compromise between the two arises in the social contract context. As was noted in Chapter 2, if the contractors, as Rawls supposes, aim 'to win for themselves the highest index of primary social goods' they will, under plausible assumptions on incentives, choose a significantly egalitarian outcome if they are infinitely risk averse and a more libertarian one if they are risk neutral. In this setting, then, the identification of some most appropriate point in the liberty–equality spectrum reduces, somewhat unsatisfactorily, to the specification of the assumed degree of risk aversion of the contractors. (Although this does not immediately fit into the Rawlsian framework, if the contractors have an intermediary degree of risk aversion and are presumed to value liberty in a non-instrumental way, as well as valuing their holdings of primary goods, they would tend to choose an outcome more towards the libertarian end of the spectrum.)

However, Arrow's theorem, reinterpreted, underlines the difficulty of specifying some most satisfactory theory of justice, and thus of identifying some most appropriate point in the liberty-equality spectrum. Since self-ownership is a cornerstone of liberty, this is given specific focus in Cohen's claim that 'anyone who supports equality of condition must oppose (full) self-ownership, even in a world in which rights over external resources have been equalized'.[10] As Otsuka expresses it,

> One can have either self-ownership or equality only at the cost of the virtual abandonment of the other. ... Nozick's *modus ponens* is Cohen's *modus tollens*, since Cohen draws the conclusion that self-ownership should give way to make room for equality, whereas Nozick draws the opposite conclusion that equality should yield to self-ownership.[11]

In an absolute sense, it seems hard to disagree with Cohen. There may, however, be some room for compromise. From one end of the spectrum equality of resources moves in that direction, particularly in making Rawlsian egalitarianism more ambition-sensitive without at the same time making it more endowment-sensitive.

From the other end of the spectrum some versions of common ownership also move in that direction. This is particularly the case for versions that embody rectification of past injustice: as Nozick accepts 'although to introduce socialism as the punishment for our sins would be to go too far, past injustices might be so great as to make necessary in the short run a more extensive state in order to rectify them'.[12]

If an accommodation is to be found it will necessarily be found towards the centre of the liberty-equality spectrum, that is, in equality of resources or in common ownership theories. Given the greater internal problems of the former, the latter may prove to be the more fruitful. However, common ownership theories are diverse, so this does not provide a complete prescription. But as Nozick reminds us, 'there is room for words on subjects other than last words'.[13]

Notes

1 Steiner (1994), page 262.
2 Otsuka (1998), page 89.
3 Sen (2009), page 5.
4 Sen (2009), page 8.
5 Sen (2009), pages 11–13.
6 Sen (2009), page 9.
7 Sen (2009), page 16.
8 Arrow (2012), chapter 5.
9 Allingham (1999), chapter 6, for example.
10 Cohen (1995), page 72.
11 Otsuka (1998), page 65.
12 Nozick (1974), page 231.
13 Nozick (1974), page xii.

BIBLIOGRAPHY

Allingham, M. (1999) *Rational Choice*, London: Macmillan.
——(2002) *Choice Theory: A Very Short Introduction*, Oxford: Oxford University Press.
Allingham, M. (ed) (2006) *Rational Choice Theory: Critical Concepts in the Social Sciences*, London: Routledge.
Anderson, E.S. (1999) 'What is the point of equality?', *Ethics*, 109: 287–337.
Aristotle (ND/1999), *Nicomachean Ethics*, translated by T. Irwin (second edition), Indianapolis, IN: Hackett.
Arneson, R. (1989) 'Equality and equal opportunity for welfare', *Philosophical Studies*, 56: 77–93.
——(1991) 'Lockean self-ownership: towards a demolition', *Political Studies*, 39: 36–54.
——(2008) 'Rawls, responsibility and distributive justice', in Fleurbaey, Salles, and Weymark (2008), 80–107.
Arrow, K.J. (1973) 'Some ordinalist-utilitarian notes on Rawls's theory of justice', *Journal of Philosophy*, 70: 245–63.
——(2012) *Social Choice and Individual Values* (third edition), New Haven, CT: Yale University Press.
Bader, R.M. and Meadowcroft, J. (eds) (2011) *The Cambridge Companion to Nozick's Anarchy, State, and Utopia*, Cambridge: Cambridge University Press.
Barry, B. (1989) *Theories of Justice*, volume 1, Berkeley, CA: University of California Press.
Bentham, J. (1843) *The Works of Jeremy Bentham*, volume 2, editor J. Bowring, Edinburgh: Tait.
Brody, B. (1983) 'Redistribution without egalitarianism', *Social Philosophy and Policy*, 1: 71–87.
Brown, A. (2009) *Ronald Dworkin's Theory of Equality: Domestic and Global Perspectives*, Basingstoke: Macmillan.
Christman, J. (1991) 'Self-ownership, equality, and the structure of property rights', *Political Theory*, 19: 28–46.
Cohen, G.A. (1983) 'The structure of proletarian unfreedom', *Philosophy & Public Affairs*, 12: 3–33.
——(1986) 'Self-ownership, world-ownership, and equality', in Lucash (1986), 108–35.
——(1989) 'On the currency of egalitarian justice', *Ethics*, 99: 906–44.
——(1995) *Self-Ownership, Freedom, and Equality*, Cambridge: Cambridge University Press.
——(1997) 'Where the action is: on the site of distributive justice', *Philosophy & Public Affairs*, 26: 3–30.
Davis, L. (1976) 'Comments on Nozick's entitlement theory', *Journal of Philosophy*, 73: 836–44.
Debreu, G. (1959) *Theory of Value*, New Haven, CT: Yale University Press.

Dworkin, R. (1977) *Taking Rights Seriously*, London: Duckworth.
——(1981) 'What is equality? Part 2: equality of resources', *Philosophy & Public Affairs*, 10: 283–345.
Elster J. and Roemer, J.E. (eds) (1991) *Interpersonal Comparisons of Well-Being*, Cambridge: Cambridge University Press.
Fleurbaey, M., Salles, S. and Weymark, J.A. (eds) (2008) *Justice, Political Liberalism, and Utilitarianism*, Cambridge: Cambridge University Press.
Freeman, S. (ed) (2003) *The Cambridge Companion to Rawls*, Cambridge: Cambridge University Press.
Fried, B. (2004) 'Left-libertarianism: a review essay', *Philosophy & Public Affairs*, 32: 66–92.
——(2011) 'Does Nozick have a theory of property rights?', in Bader and Meadowcroft (2011), 230–52.
Gaus, G. and D'Agostino, F. (eds) (2012) *The Routledge Companion to Social and Political Philosophy*, London: Routledge.
George, H. (1897) *The Condition of Labor: An Open Letter to Pope Leo XIII*, New York: Sterling.
Gibbard, A. (1976) 'Natural property rights', *Nous*, 10: 77–86.
Griffin, J. (1991) 'Against the taste model', in Elster and Roemer (1991), 45–69.
Grunebaum, J. (1987) *Private Ownership*, New York: Routledge.
Halévy, É. (1904) *La Formation du Radicalisme Philosophique*, volume 3, Paris: Alcan.
Hammond, P.J. (1991) 'Interpersonal comparisons of utility: why and how they are and should be made', in Elster and Roemer (1991), 200–254.
Hardin, G. (1968) 'The tragedy of the commons', *Science*, 162: 1243–48.
Harsanyi, J. (1953) 'Cardinal utility in welfare economics and in the theory of risk-taking', *Journal of Political Economy*, 61: 434–35.
——(1977) 'Morality and the theory of rational behavior', *Social Research*, 44; reprinted in Sen and Williams (1982), 39–62.
Hayek, F.A. (1976) *The Mirage of Social Justice*, London: Routledge.
Heath, J. (2004) 'Dworkin's auction', *Politics, Philosophy and Economics*, 3: 313–451.
Hicks, J.R. (1946) *Value and Capital: An Inquiry into some Fundamental Principles of Economic Theory*, Oxford: Clarendon Press.
Honoré, A.M. (1987) *Making Law Bind: Essays Legal and Philosophical*, Oxford: Clarendon Press.
Hume, D. (1739/2000) *A Treatise of Human Nature*, edited by D.F. and M.J. Norton, Oxford: Oxford University Press.
——(1751/1998) *An Enquiry Concerning the Principles of Morals*, edited by T.L. Beauchamp, Oxford: Oxford University Press.
Hunt, L. (1998) *British Low Culture*, London: Routledge.
Kirzner, I. (1978) 'Entrepreneurship, entitlement, and economic justice', *Eastern Economic Journal*, 4: 9–25; reprinted in Vallentyne and Steiner (2000), 191–213.
Klein, M. (1957) *Envy and Gratitude: A Study of Unconscious Forces*, London: Tavistock.
Kreps, D. (1988) *Notes on the Theory of Choice*, Boulder, CO: Westview.
Kuflik, A. (1982) 'Process and end-state in the theory of economic justice', *Social Theory and Practice*, 8: 73–94.
Kymlicka, W. (2002) *Contemporary Political Philosophy* (second edition), Oxford: Oxford University Press.
Locke, J. (1689/1988) *Two Treatises of Government*, edited by P. Laslett, Cambridge: Cambridge University Press.
——(1690/2008) *An Essay Concerning Human Understanding*, edited by P. Phemister, Oxford: Oxford University Press.
Lucash, F. (ed) (1986) *Justice and Equality Here and Now*, Ithaca, NY: Cornell University Press.
MacIntyre, A.C. (2007) *After Virtue: A Study in Moral Theory* (third edition), London: Duckworth.
Macleod, C. (1998) *Liberalism, Justice, and Markets: A Critique of Liberal Equality*, Oxford: Oxford University Press.

Mandle, J. (2009) *Rawls's A Theory of Justice*, Cambridge: Cambridge University Press.

Martin, R. (2012) 'The difference principle', in Gaus and D'Agostino (2012), 401–11.

McMurrin, S.M. (ed) (1980) *The Tanner Lectures on Human Values*, Cambridge: Cambridge University Press.

Meadowcroft, J. (2011) 'Nozick's critique of Rawls: distribution, entitlement, and the assumptive world of *A Theory of Justice*', in Bader and Meadowcroft (2011), 168–96.

Mill, J.S. (1865) *On Liberty* (people's edition), London: Longman.

Nagel, T. (1975) 'Libertarianism without foundations', *Yale Law Review*, 85: 136–49.

Narveson, J. (2001) *The Libertarian Ideal*, Ontario: Broadview.

Nozick, R. (1974) *Anarchy, State, and Utopia*, Oxford: Blackwell.

——(1989) *The Examined Life*, New York: Simon and Schuster.

Nussbaum, M. (2006) *Frontiers of Justice: Disability, Nationality, Species Membership*, Cambridge, MA: Harvard University Press.

O'Neill, O. (1976) 'Nozick's entitlements', *Inquiry*, 19: 468–81.

Orwell, G. (1937) *The Road to Wigan Pier*, London: Gollancz.

——(1938) *Homage to Catalonia*, London: Secker and Warburg.

Otsuka, M. (1998) 'Self-ownership and equality: a Lockean reconciliation', *Philosophy & Public Affairs*, 27: 65–92.

Paul, J. (ed) (1982) *Reading Nozick: Essays on Anarchy, State, and Utopia*, Oxford: Blackwell.

Pazner, E.A. and Schmeidler, D. (1974) 'A difficulty in the concept of fairness', *Review of Economic Studies*, 41: 441–43.

Pettit, P. (1980) *Judging Justice: An Introduction to Contemporary Political Philosophy*, London: Routledge.

Rawls, J. (1975) 'A Kantian conception of equality', *Cambridge Review*, 96: 94–99; reprinted in Rawls (1999b), 254–66.

——(1989) 'The domain of the political and overlapping consensus', *New York University Law Review*, 64: 233–55; reprinted in Rawls (1999b), 473–96.

——(1999a) *A Theory of Justice* (revised edition), Oxford: Oxford University Press.

——(1999b) *Collected Papers*, edited by S. Freeman, Cambridge, MA: Harvard University Press.

——(2001) *Justice as Fairness: A Restatement*, edited by E. Kelly, Cambridge, MA: Harvard University Press.

——(2005) *Political Liberalism* (expanded edition), New York: Columbia University Press.

Rignano, E. (1901) *Di un Socialismo in Accordo colla Dottrina Economica Liberale*, Turin: Fratelli Bocca.

Roemer, J.E. (1985) 'Equality of talent', *Economics and Philosophy*, 1: 151–87.

——(1996) *Theories of Distributive Justice*, Cambridge, MA: Harvard University Press.

Rothbard, M.N. (1973) *For a New Liberty*, New York: Macmillan.

Ryan, C. (1977) 'Yours, mine and ours: property rights and individual liberty', *Ethics*, 87: 126–41.

Sandel, M.J. (1998) *Liberalism and the Limits of Justice* (second edition), Cambridge: Cambridge University Press.

——(2009) *Justice: What's the Right Thing to Do?*, Allen Lane: London.

Savage, L.J. (1954) *The Foundations of Statistics*, New York: Wiley.

Scanlon, T. (1986) 'Equality of resources and equality of welfare: a forced marriage?', *Ethics*, 97: 111–18.

——(1991) 'The moral basis of interpersonal comparisons', in Elster and Roemer (1991), 17–44.

Sen, A. (1970a) *Collective Choice and Social Welfare*, London: Oliver & Boyd.

——(1970b) 'The impossibility of a Paretian liberal', *Journal of Political Economy*, 78: 152–57; reprinted in Allingham (2006), volume 4, 15–20.

——(1980) 'Equality of what?' in McMurrin (1980), 197–220.

——(1987) *The Standard of Living*, edited by G. Hawthorn, Cambridge: Cambridge University Press.

——(2005) 'Human rights and capabilities', *Journal of Human Development*, 6: 151–66.

——(2009) *The Idea of Justice*, London: Allen Lane.

Sen, A. and Williams. B. (eds) (1982) *Utilitarianism and Beyond*, Cambridge: Cambridge University Press.

Sidgwick, H. (1874/1981) *The Methods of Ethics*, Indianapolis, IN: Hackett.

Smith, A. (1759/2002) *The Theory of Moral Sentiments*, edited by K. Haakonssen, Cambridge: Cambridge University Press.

Steiner, H. (1977) 'Justice and entitlement', *Ethics*, 87: 150–52

——(1978) 'Nozick on appropriation', *Mind*, 87: 109–10.

——(1994) *An Essay on Rights*, Cambridge, MA: Blackwell.

——(2011) Sharing mother nature's gifts: a reply to Quong and Miller, *Journal of Political Philosophy*, 19: 110–23.

——(2012) 'Left libertarianism', in Gaus and D'Agostino (2012), 412–21.

Sterne, L. (1761/1980) *The Life and Opinions of Tristram Shandy, Gentleman*, edited by H. Anderson, New York: Norton.

Taylor, R.S. (2004) 'A Kantian defense of self-ownership', *Journal of Political Philosophy*, 1: 65–78.

Vallentyne, P. (1998) 'Critical notice of G.A. Cohen's *Self-Ownership, Freedom, and Equality*', *Canadian Journal of Philosophy*, 28: 609–26.

——(2000) 'Introduction: left-libertarianism – a primer', in Vallentyne and Steiner (2000), 1–20.

——(2005) 'Debate: capabilities versus opportunities for wellbeing', *Journal of Political Philosophy*, 13: 359–71.

——(2011) 'Nozick's libertarian theory of justice', in Bader and Meadowcroft (2011), 145–67.

Vallentyne, P. and Steiner, H. (eds) (2000) *Left Libertarianism and Its Critics: The Contemporary Debate*, Basingstoke: Palgrave.

Van Parijs, P. (1995) *Real Freedom for All: What (if Anything) Can Justify Capitalism*, Oxford: Clarendon Press.

——(2003) 'Difference principles', in Freeman (2003), 200–240.

Varian, H. (1976) 'Two problems in the theory of fairness', *Journal of Public Economics*, 5: 249–60.

Walras, L. (1896/1990) *Études d'Économie Sociale*, editor P. Dockès, Paris: Economica.

Williams, B. (1982) 'The minimal state', in Paul (1982), 27–36.

Wolff, J. (1991) *Robert Nozick: Property, Justice, and the Minimal State*, Cambridge: Polity.

INDEX